COPPER AND THE TREE FROG

COPPER AND THE TREE FROG

THE NIGHT HERON NABBING

MIKE JONES

Illustrated by
LEYSAN SOVETNIKOVA

THAXTON PRESS, LLC

ISBN 978-0-9890046-4-0 (Hardcover)

ISBN 978-0-9890046-5-7 (Paperback)

ISBN 978-0-9890046-6-4 (E-book)

Library of Congress Control Number: 2020911652

This is a work of fiction. All characters, places, dialogue, and incidents are drawn from the author's imagination or are used fictitiously and are not to be construed as real. Any resemblance to actual persons, living or dead, business establishments, or events is entirely coincidental.

Cover art and illustrations by Leysan Sovetnikova

Published by Thaxton Press, LLC

P.O. Box 80363

Charleston, SC 29416

www.copperandthetreefrog.com

For Monica, forever my true companion

CONTENTS

FIRE THE KITTEN CANNONBALLS!

H er name was Copper, but she didn't know that quite yet.

That was just one of many things about life that Copper hadn't learned. After all, her entire world was the cozy kitten community room at Chucktown Cats & Hounds, an animal shelter in Charleston, South Carolina. If a kitten had to be living in a shelter, there was no better place to be. She had towers to climb, hammocks to lie in, and oodles of toys to swat around. When no toy was available, Copper enjoyed ambushing unsuspecting kittens from behind the climbing tower. She had strong ninja skills for such a young feline.

Across the hallway, in the seasoned seniors' suite, lived the older cats. Each room had a wood-framed door with chicken coop wire stretched across it, so humans could peek inside without frisky felines trying to make a break for it. Sometimes in the wee hours of the morning, Copper would hang out by the kitten community room door and try to strike up a conversation with the older cats across the hall. But they would just stare at her blankly or lie down and show her their backsides. They seemed like a sad and grumpy group in the seasoned seniors' suite.

On one of her late-night prowls, Copper noticed a white calico with orange and black patches staring into the kitten room. She hadn't seen this cat before. "Hi there!" Copper greeted the newcomer with an enthusiastic grin that seemed wider than her face.

The calico flattened her ears, bared her teeth, and gave such a fearsome hiss that Copper turned and ran in a panic, slamming headfirst into a three-story kitty tower and hurling two groggy kitten cannonballs into nearby hammocks chock full of even more sleeping kitties. The tower crashed into a feeding station, and a mushroom cloud of kibble and water enveloped the area. A frenzy of fleeing kittens formed, and the world's cutest stampede thundered through the once-tranquil kitten community room. Kittens skidded across the slick floor, colliding with one another as feeding stations and kitty towers toppled like dominoes.

A single calico hiss had set off a chain reaction that left a trail of destruction in the kitten room. Climbing towers lay crumpled in rubble of scattered soggy cat food. An eerie sound like rain hitting pavement filled the room as the slurping herd of soaking wet kittens frantically attempted to dry themselves with their tongues. One kitten was left to air-dry because he had somehow caught his paw in a hammock. For the rest of the night, he sat on the floor with one leg held up like he was trying to ask the teacher a question but couldn't get her attention.

In the morning, a very confused group of shelter employees arrived and found a haze of cat food dust clouding the rays of sunlight streaming into the kitten community room. They quickly freed the little guy who had his paw stuck in a hammock. Because the entire room was a disaster area and all the kittens were covered in fine cat food particles, the shelter employees decided to give each kitten a bath. That was the day Copper realized two things about herself. She wasn't very fond of calico cats, and she really, really, really hated baths.

Despite the catastrophe from the night before, Copper decided to visit the door of the kitten community room again the next evening. She wasn't sure what she would do if the calico was there, but she couldn't contain her curiosity about the grown-up cats across the hallway. Still, as she pussyfooted her way to the door all she could think was, "Please don't be the calico, please don't be the calico."

To her great relief, the door across the hallway was calico-cat free. Instead, an old, green-eyed tomcat was there, lounging on his side. His fur was solid black except for a lightbulb-shaped patch of white on his chest. At that moment, Copper decided to say hello and not let one bad experience stop her from trying to make new friends. She mustered up her courage, prepared for the worst, and hoped for the best.

Fortunately, the black tomcat set her at ease by speaking first. "Why hello there, little one," he said as he licked the side of his paw and brushed it behind a tattered ear. "I must admit I've cooked up a disaster or two in my time, but that was a colossal commotion you caused last night."

"Umm, yeah that was a little embarrassing. I don't think the calico liked me."

"Don't let it bother you, kid. That was Callie and she does not play well with others. Somehow, she keeps getting herself adopted but her humans always bring her back." He casually looked over his shoulder and added, "Hey Callie, what's your record for longest adoption? About two weeks?"

Just then, hissing arose from somewhere in the back of the seasoned seniors' suite.

Copper didn't want to pile any more abuse on the calico. "I'm sure she simply needs the right human to come along."

Another loud hiss echoed throughout the room, this time interrupted by the unmistakable gagging sound of Callie the calico with a hairball caught in her throat. It sounded like a toilet beginning to flush. Copper tried to hold it together in front of her new friend, but a small giggle escaped anyway. The black cat sat upright and gazed across at Copper, his grin revealing that he thought the unfortunately timed hairball was hilarious too. "My name is Sarge," he said, "and I'm guessing you don't know your name yet."

"Nice to meet you, Sarge!" Copper hadn't thought about knowing her name before. "How do I get a name?" she asked.

Sarge opened his mouth to reply. But before he could get a word out, one final extra-strength hack came from the room behind him, followed by the sound of something disgusting hitting the tiled floor. Callie's Operation Hairball Launch had been a success. Without acknowledging the grossness behind him, Sarge continued, "When your humans adopt you, they'll take you home and give you a name."

"How will I know the name they've given me? The humans here talk to us all the time, but I can't understand a word they're saying."

"They'll say the same word to you a bunch in human language," Sarge explained. "At first, you'll think they aren't too bright because they keep repeating themselves, but they honestly have more of a vocabulary than you think. The word that you hear more than any other is going to be your name."

Copper sat on her hind legs and wrapped her tail around her paws. After hearing Sarge's explanation, it occurred to her that she might already have a name. She opened her eyes wide and perked her oversized ears. "I think my name is Kitty," she declared.

Sarge nodded as if he was expecting Copper to say that. "That's a word humans use when they don't know our names. You've got the right idea, though. You've heard 'Kitty' a lot, but when you get adopted, you will need to listen for a different, new word that your humans keep saying." He rubbed his face against the wire mesh on the door as he added, "Don't get that confused with 'no-no' though."

Copper tilted her head, which is the cat equivalent of saying, "Say what?" Like all cats, Copper was a little lazy, so if she could say an entire sentence with a simple head-move, she was all about that.

Sarge smirked as he clarified, "No-no is what humans say when they want you to speed up whatever you're doing. If you are sharpening your claws on the couch, jumping on the kitchen table, or sprinting through the house in the middle of the night and they say 'no-no,' then they want you to do it faster. Some humans will even come running at you or throw a pillow to speed you up."

"Wow, humans do some weird things," marveled Copper.

"They sure do," Sarge agreed. "And I only know a little about them. You'll be adopted soon and then you'll truly find out how weird they are."

"Why do you think I'll get adopted soon?"

Sarge stretched out on his belly with his paws in front of him. He looked over at the little orange tabby with stripes and swirls going every which way. "You're a kitten, and you are cute. Humans will come running for that combo like cats to a bowl of wet food."

The mention of delicious canned wet food immediately caused Copper's mind to drift off, although that wasn't out of the ordinary. Copper was easily distracted. The shelter vet called this condition Acute Feline Distractitis.

Copper's Distract Facts

If you've ever had a cat as a pet, seen a cat at a friend's house, or watched a cat video, you know they can get distracted easily. A cat can be stalking a ferocious cricket or preparing a sneak attack on the family dog when suddenly it will stop and lick a random spot on its side for no good reason. Acute Feline Distractitis is not a real thing, but if it was, Copper would definitely suffer from it.

Throughout her adventures, Copper will meet many amazing creatures. Each creature she meets is a type of animal you might be able to see around homes, schools, parks, beaches, cities, environmental education centers, or lots of other fun outdoor places. The animals you'll see in your surroundings are just as amazing as those that Copper meets, and her Distract Facts share some interesting things to look for when you see them. So, when you see the paws, it's a chance to pause and learn a little more about nature.

Learn more at distractfacts.com.

COPPER'S EYES glazed over as thoughts of yummy wet food flooded her brain. Her mouth hung open, with a bit of drool forming on her lips. She was imagining the delightful pop of an aluminum can lid and the savory aroma of juicy mystery meat chunks sliding from the can when Sarge snapped her out of the trance. "Plus, you are friendly and playful. Humans love to see that when they visit the shelter." Sarge glanced over his shoulder again and added, "That doesn't seem to come naturally to *some* cats."

Copper braced herself for another of Callie's frightful hisses, but instead a long, low growl came from the unseen corners of Sarge's room. Apparently, Callie had decided against further hissing. Better not to risk another awkward hairball incident. "That Callie is a furry ball of meanness," Sarge continued. "She's been returned so many times the workers here have started calling her Comeback Callie." Sarge ducked as a calico paw swooshed over his head from just beyond the door frame. Despite his verbal jabs, Copper had a feeling Sarge was fond of Callie. He obviously knew a lot about her history.

"How long have you lived here?" Copper asked as Sarge kept a watchful eye for another swipe from Callie.

"I just got here yesterday." Sarge's naturally mischievous grin disappeared as he added, "They think I'm a stray."

"What's a stray?" questioned Copper.

"A stray is a house animal that has no home. But I'm no stray, little one. The world is my home."

Copper stared into Sarge's emerald eyes. The gray haze wrapping his pupils made him look both wise and tired. "So, you've never had your own humans?" she asked.

Sarge yawned wide, revealing a couple of missing teeth, and further explained, "I had a human, but that was only for a short while and a long time ago. That was before—" Sarge stopped talking when he realized Copper had disappeared. When he heard litter box scratching coming from the kitten room, Sarge chuckled as he stretched and walked gingerly to one of the plushy beds in the seasoned seniors' suite. "Sometimes you have to answer the call of nature," he said softly to himself. "I was just about to tell her all about that."

2

NEVER TRUST YOUR TAIL

The next day, Copper spent most of her time tackling kittens and swatting crinkly toys across the floor. She was having too much fun to get in a standard nap schedule, so she merely settled for morning, mid-morning, pre-lunch, post-lunch, mid-afternoon, and late-afternoon naptimes. Once, between her afternoon naps, she thought about Sarge, but when she strolled to the screen door, he wasn't there. Instead, there was a gray tabby with white sock-like feet sitting at the doorway to the seasoned seniors' suite.

She tried to say hello to the sock-wearing cat, but he sat there blinking like he didn't hear her or didn't know how to respond to a simple hello. Copper was about to ask him if he knew Sarge, when she noticed something trying to sneak up behind her. It was orange and stripy and flicked gently side-to-side. She inched toward the strange creature and it moved away from her, mirroring her moves with precision. It was like the creature knew she saw it, but it wanted to stay close anyway.

Copper continued to circle toward it, and it continued to

circle away from her, never getting any closer or any further away. This was a cunning enemy following her, but she knew she would get the better of this hunt. Leaping at the creature, Copper seized it in her mighty kitten paws. The great huntress had caught her prey.

Then she realized it was her own tail.

Copper quickly released her death grip on her tail, hoping that Mr. Sockfeet hadn't seen her embarrassing performance. When she twirled around and looked across the hallway, she found Sarge sitting there instead.

"Ah, the old 'I thought my tail was a snake that looks exactly like me and was sneaking up behind me' mistake." Sarge laughed sympathetically. "Don't worry about it, kid. We've all done it at least once or twice." He glanced with suspicion at his own tail.

"It was like it had a mind all its own! I *know* I wasn't moving it," Copper said with eyes wide as quarters.

"Oh yes, I know the feeling. Like I said, it happens to the best of us. No need to explain yourself."

"Thanks, Sarge." Copper eyeballed her tail once more before turning back to the old tomcat. "Hey, that reminds me. I meant to ask you a question last night before I had to uh, take care of some business. Was Sarge the name your human gave you?"

"No, I stopped answering to that name many years ago. Sometimes—"

"Watch out!" Copper shouted.

Sarge wheeled around and his tail puffed up like a big angry cloud on the end of his butt.

Poofy Tails

Cats puff up their tails when they are frightened or feel threatened. It's an instinctive reaction to make themselves look bigger to whoever or whatever is threatening them. They can poof out their tails to twice the normal size. Fortunately, humans can't do this, or else we would be replacing our pants far too often.

Learn more at distractfacts.com/poofytails.

As soon as Sarge saw Callie standing behind him, his tail shrank to its normal pencil-like shape. Callie strutted up to the screen door and glared at Copper. "Why don't you go ahead and tell her the name your human gave you?" Callie sneered at Sarge without turning her gaze from Copper.

"Why don't we tell the story about how you got that nice little brown spot under your eye?" Sarge calmly countered. "I think everyone here would enjoy that explosive tale."

Under Callie's left eye, Copper caught a glimpse of a brown streak which looked sort of like a rotten banana. Callie mumbled something and slipped out of sight, but Copper still felt like the calico's eyes were watching her somehow.

"Sorry about that," said Sarge. "Callie and I go way back, and there are lots of stories we could tell on each other. To answer your question, Sarge is the name my animal friends gave me years ago. House animals get names from their humans, but most other animals get names from their parents or friends. A few of us lucky ones get names from both."

"When you say other animals, you mean like the dogs down the hallway?" Copper asked.

Sarge smiled. "You don't know it yet because you haven't been out of this shelter, but the world is much bigger than the little parts where we make our homes. Everywhere is not the same as your somewhere. There are animals and places out there that are simply amazing. When you look, you see."

Copper had a hard time imagining a world outside the kitten community room. Sarge had the most fantastic stories to tell about the incredible places where he'd traveled and some of the fascinating animals he had met. Copper spent the next few hours asking him question after question. Trying to picture the places and the creatures Sarge talked about was difficult for Copper. Until now, she had only seen cats, humans, and the occasional dog passing by.

There were several interruptions during all their hours of talking. A few of them weren't even Copper's fault. The shelter workers were busier than usual, and they scurried in and out of the cat rooms, spraying something on the windows and wiping the stuff right back off with towels. Copper thought that was a rather odd thing to do. She also noticed that the workers picked things up off the floor and moved them to other places in the room. Her stomach rumbled as she watched one worker cram a jar of kitty treats into a jam-packed cabinet.

Copper thoughtfully reasoned that the shelter workers must want to rearrange things to make the room look different. Thanks to her natural desire to help, an idea popped into her head. She skipped over to one of the silvery food bowls, plucked out a piece of food, and swatted it across the floor to a new spot.

Very proud of her first try at helping, Copper decided that the food looked great in the new spot, and it was also much more convenient for the kittens on that side of the room who wanted a snack. She decided to move the rest of it. And with that, Copper began to shovel out every bit of food from the bowl and swat it to a new location. She was having fun and being helpful at the same time!

The other kittens didn't have the same natural desire to be as helpful as Copper, but tiny cat food pieces flying across the floor captured their attention. Within seconds, every kitten was pouncing and swatting food from one end of the room to the other. A shelter worker who was walking by snatched open the door and cried, "No-no!"

Thanks to Sarge, Copper knew exactly what to do.

"They want us to go faster, everyone! Let's move these chunks of food as fast as we can!"

To the shelter worker's ears, this sounded something like a loud "Mew!!"

Copper began slapping kibble like a human trying to get a

bee out of his face. Kittens scrambled everywhere at lightning speed. Bits of kitty food skidded across the floor like leaves in a tornado, driven by a funnel cloud of kittens. Lunging for one of the kittens, the shelter worker stumbled over a scratcher toy with a ball hidden inside. The toy flipped over, the ball catapulted across the room, and the shelter worker grabbed a cabinet door to catch herself. The door to the overstuffed cabinet flew open, releasing the jar of chewy kitty treats which crashed to the floor, spewing treats everywhere.

Another staff member heard the clamor and arrived to find her bewildered coworker standing in the room with cat food splattered from corner to corner, kittens sprinting in every direction and battling to snag kitty treats, and one fluffy white kitten swatting around the ball that had been freed from its scratcher toy prison. Only one climbing tower remained upright, and Copper jumped to the top platform to survey the remodeling project she had done with her fellow kittens. She purred loudly with contentment. The room certainly did look different! She knew the shelter workers must be very happy that the kittens had helped. For some reason, though, they didn't look as happy as she had expected.

When shelter employees began sweeping up and putting items back where they were before, Copper was astonished. It was the same kind of thing they had done with the windows. Spray something on and then wipe it right back off. No doubt about it. Humans were weird. Copper hopped down from the climbing tower to see if Sarge had any idea why they behaved like that.

Dodging another shelter employee as he entered the room with a broom and a long-handled dustpan, Copper walked over to the screen door of the kitten community room. While Copper had been helping the shelter staff rearrange things,

Sarge had dozed off by the door to his own room with a paw resting over his eyes. The latch on the kitten room door clicked shut, and Sarge drew back his paw to see Copper trying to lick an itchy spot below her chin.

"That's one thing your humans will be good for," Sarge said with the gravelly voice of someone who has just awakened from a blue-ribbon nap. "When you've got an itch out of reach, all you have to do is jump right in the middle of whatever a human is doing and give them a little bump with your head. They'll scratch the top of your head or under your chin without you having to tell them anything. They're pretty easy to train."

Copper stopped her quest to scratch the unscratchable. "That's good to hear. Hopefully, my human will have a good rough tongue. That spot at the top of my head itches all the time and I had to get the white fluffy kitten to lick it for me earlier today. I noticed one of the shelter ladies smiling big when she saw that. I guess she was happy that she didn't have to do it."

"What? No, humans don't use their tongues. They scratch with their hands. She was probably smiling because you were doing something cute. When they are grinning at you or you hear them say something like 'Awwww,' it means you are doing something cute. You can get them to do anything you want when you do something cute."

That made sense to Copper. She had already begun to suspect cats had the ability to control humans. One time, she had been sleeping in a kitty hammock with her paws in the air and a human had scratched her belly without her asking. It did seem like they were easy to train.

"Listen," said Sarge, "you've probably noticed a lot of activity around here today. That means they're getting the place ready for a whole bunch of humans to come in and adopt pets. This may be the last time we get to talk, and I wanted to let you know I really like you, kid. Even after crabby Callie lashed out at you just for being friendly, you were still kind enough to say she just needs to find the right humans. I can tell you've got a good heart. We could use a few more animals like you in this world."

Copper had been excited at the idea of getting her own humans, but she hadn't thought about leaving her new friend behind. She liked Sarge. It made her sad to think she might not see him again. "Is there a chance you and I could be adopted by the same people?" she asked.

"Humans who come looking for a kitten aren't usually interested in an old feline like myself," said Sarge. "I'm not likely to be adopted at all."

Copper didn't like hearing Sarge talk like that. "Well, maybe I'll do something to keep from getting adopted, like turn off my cuteness so they won't notice me. I like it here. It's comfortable and I wouldn't mind staying."

Sarge laughed and his smile had a warmth that Copper could almost feel on her fur across the hallway. "I don't think you could turn off the cuteness even if you tried, little one, and you don't need to stay here simply because you are comfortable. Never be content being content."

"What do you mean by that?"

"I mean never pass up the chance for a new adventure. It can be scary at first, because it might be something you aren't used to, like having your own humans. They can be weird, but I think you'll be glad you have them. You'll never know until you go on that first adventure."

"First adventure?" asked Copper. "Do you think I'll be going on adventures like the ones you've had?"

"Every creature has its own adventures in life," said Sarge. "The adventures that come your way will be different from mine. Just be ready when the moment comes."

Copper perked up her ears. The sound of tiny padded feet hitting the floor behind her meant a kitten had vacated a kitty hammock, and a nice pre-warmed bed was immediately available. A heated bed was worth fighting for in a room full of cats, so Copper wanted to stake her claim quickly.

"Gonna nap, chat with you later," she muttered as she hurried over to the hammock.

Her abrupt exit didn't offend Sarge. A little more napping sounded pretty good to him as well. He had started to feel a lot of the aches and pains that come with being a twelve-year-old cat since his arrival at the shelter. All this sitting around wasn't doing him any good.

He scanned the room for an available plushy bed, but all of them were taken. Along one wall was a series of crisscrossing shelves arranged like steps for the cats to climb. On the top shelf, next to a small rectangular window, sat Callie. She was flicking her tail up and down and making a strange chattering sound toward a crow on the window ledge. Sarge thought the crow looked familiar and figured its presence would make the cantankerous calico even grumpier. One more thing to make his stay in the seasoned seniors' suite a little less pleasant.

What's with the Chatter?

Some cats will make an unusual clicking and whining sound when they see a bird or squirrel outside a window. Experts have different ideas as to why cats do this, but the general theory points to a cat's hunting instincts. The cat is either signaling frustration because it can't get to its potential prey, or it is announcing how much it would like to kill that thing outside the window. In Callie's case, always assume the latter.

Learn more at distractfacts.com/catchatter.

SARGE SETTLED onto a blanket near the back of the room. The windows there stretched from floor to ceiling. He warmed himself in the last sunbeam of the day and watched one of the shelter workers walk a dog down the sidewalk. As Sarge's eyelids became heavier than his desire to keep them open, he drifted off for some much-needed rest.

The shelter employees went home for the day and soon sunbeams turned to moonbeams. Copper got up a few times as usual during the evening and checked for Sarge at the door. When she didn't find him there, she returned to snoozing or trying to tempt another kitten into a wrestling match. Late in the night, Copper heard a commotion coming from the seasoned seniors' suite. Crashes and multiple cats yowling like a choir of old creaky doors echoed through the space, followed by an eerie silence. Copper ran to the door, calling Sarge's name.

There was no answer.

She stayed there, watching and calling for Sarge until the sunbeams returned, and the shelter staff arrived for the Saturday morning shift. More humans began to appear shortly after the staff had arrived. Most of them made a beeline down the hallway to the dog section. Copper got on her hind legs and stood tall against the screen to watch them go by. She was also hoping to get a good look into the seasoned seniors' suite, which was busy with workers carrying in brooms and dust-pans like they did in the kitten room after she had helped rearrange things. Finally, one of the workers walked out carrying something that looked like a cat in his arms.

As she stood there with her paws on the screen door, Copper called Sarge's name again just as a family of four humans arrived. The young boy and girl saw a cute orange tabby kitten, dark orange stripes and swirls going every which way, standing on her hind legs and meowing at the door. Their hearts melted. They carried her to the front desk, and as Sarge had predicted, Copper became a member of a family that very day.

She purred as the boy cradled her and the girl stroked her head while their parents talked to the shelter worker at the desk. The children kept saying the word "Copper" as they showered attention on her. The shelter worker repeated the word as she wrote up some paperwork. Copper wondered if she was hearing her new name. She liked the sound of it.

Copper was both excited and sad. She was getting her own humans and she had learned her new name, but she wanted to share the news with Sarge. What had happened in the seasoned seniors' suite in the middle of the night? Why hadn't he come back to the door to talk with her at least one last time? Copper was pulled away from her thoughts as her new family loaded her into a pet carrier for the ride to her new home. When a shelter worker set the pet carrier on the counter, Copper was shocked to see a familiar cat locked in a cage behind the desk. As she left the shelter with her new family, the last thing Copper saw was Callie's fierce eyes staring at her from inside that cage.

3

TOXIC FROGS FOR DINNER

Copper loved everything about her new home. Well, everything except the family dog, Oscar. She probably could have done without him. Copper had attempted to introduce herself a few times, but the dog had faulty barking brakes. He. Never. Stopped. Barking.

Because her humans repeated it so often, Copper quickly learned Oscar's name. At first, she thought his name was "Oscar, shhhhh" but they didn't say that every time, and she finally realized his name was Oscar. She wondered why humans liked dogs so much if they were all like him.

Her humans had never lived with a cat, so they had plenty to learn. Furniture was scratched, houseplants were eaten, and embarrassing personal grooming was done openly in front of guests. And no one would ever forget the Christmas Tree Incident. Copper's family discovered that bringing home a freshly cut tree, sticking it in a bucket of water, and hanging shiny, breakable objects on it was not the best idea with an energetic cat on the loose.

Copper's time at the shelter made her even stranger than

the average cat. She would act out Sarge's adventure stories and gallop through the house jumping from couch to coffee table, to chair, to ottoman, to countertop, to fridge, and then run the whole course backwards. The usual grand finale for these crazed kitty track and field events was a collision with the wall after rounding a corner and losing traction on the hardwood floor.

Her humans figured wacky behavior was normal for a kitten, but after a year, Copper was full-grown yet still crazy. At least she had grown into her ears. Mostly.

Copper's silliness made her humans happy to have her, and she was happy to have them. She even learned a thing or two about them. Using Sarge's technique, Copper had figured out a couple of their names. The younger ones answered when the older ones called out Mason or Molly although sometimes the older humans had to repeat the word at increasing volumes before the younger ones answered. Copper supposed that was just another weird human thing.

All in all, Copper loved her humans and they catered to her every need. She was comfortable and content, but she still felt like something was missing. Thanks to Sarge, adventure was always on her mind. Unfortunately, there wasn't a whole lot of adventure to be found around her little house.

That was about to change.

It was the end of a beautiful spring day in Charleston, and Copper had enjoyed herself as usual. Earlier in the day, Molly had taken her outside with the walking harness. Copper had chased spiders and savored the feel of cool blades of grass beneath her paws. The only downside was that Molly had forgotten to take off the harness again, which meant Copper would be spending half the night trying to scratch unreachable spots on her belly.

At dusk, she loitered by one of her favorite spots, the patio door. The inside lights illuminated the patio with a soft glow like candlelight, and that always brought the moths in droves. Copper liked to swat in vain at the moths landing on the glass. She sniffed at a cool breeze wafting through the living room window. As Copper tracked a moth fluttering by, she noticed something she had never seen before.

A green tree frog was pressed against a pane of glass on her patio door.

His spindly, padded toes gripped the glass like little suction cups. A white stripe curved up from his mouth like an everlasting smile and ran the length of his body. Copper swatted at the frog, first with one paw and then the other. She lunged for a closer look, banging her nose against the glass.

"You know that is glass, right? You can't get to me," the frog yelled.

What's That Froggy in the Window?

While Copper heard him plain as day, her humans only heard the frog's natural call. It sounded like a person holding their nose and saying the word "bank" repeatedly. Go ahead and try that yourself now. I'll wait right here while you do it.

Did you try it? If you did, hopefully, you weren't in the library or you've got some explaining to do for your rather odd behavior. No matter where you were, if you tried it, you have a pretty good idea of what Copper's humans heard.

The frog on Copper's patio door is commonly called a green tree frog. The scientific name for a green tree frog is *Hyla cinerea*. You can learn more about scientific names in "The Taxonomy of *Copper and the Tree Frog*" section at the end of the book.

Green tree frogs can grow to around two inches in length and they have sticky toe pads which allow them to hang on to all sorts of things. They usually have a light racing stripe down their sides. Many also have orange or yellow speckles on their backs. While they live mostly in the southern United States, there are similar tree frogs nearly everywhere. Oh yeah, they are also green.

Learn more at distractfacts.com/riley.

"WHAT ARE you doing on my porch?" Copper asked her uninvited guest.

The tree frog rolled an eye toward her. "Your porch? I've been on this porch more than a few times and I've never seen you out here before."

"Well, I'm not usually out there," Copper conceded. Unwilling to fully give up the point, she added, "But it's my porch."

The tree frog snatched up a moth that drifted too close in its journey to the light. "Whaf's you nim?" he asked, with a mouthful of quivering moth.

"Ummm, what did you say? I'm not used to chatting with an animal who has half a freshly killed insect hanging out of his mouth."

The tree frog swallowed the moth in three gulps, thus ending for the moth an otherwise very fine evening of swirling around the porchlight.

"Sorry about that," replied the tree frog. "Gotta grab a meal when you can or else you starve, you know?"

Copper turned and looked in the kitchen at her bowl, which had a small mountain of food piled in it. She really didn't know.

"I was asking you for your name," the frog went on. "My name is Riley."

"My name is Copper," she stammered, as if she wasn't sure she was saying it right.

"Excellent! That's what they told me your name was, but I wanted to make sure I was in the right pla—" The conversation was interrupted as a blurry brown and white blob streaked past the door and the tree frog disappeared!

Copper stuck her nose to the glass and scanned the backyard. She looked from the playset at one end of the yard to the shed on the other. She was leaving those cool nose print designs on the glass that her humans always wiped away.

Copper enjoyed looking at her nose print art and trying to guess what shape it had taken. This particular one looked like a peanut, and she began to think about those roasted peanuts her humans brought home. She loved swatting around the shells whenever the little humans dropped them.

Snap out of it! thought Copper. She often had to "get her own attention" since random things distracted her. As Copper resumed her search for the frog, she noticed a slight movement in one of the oak trees. An owl was perched on a thick, low-hanging branch. This was the first time Copper had seen an owl, which meant it was also the first time she had seen an owl with two green legs hanging out of its beak.

"Hey!" shouted Copper. Her humans heard something more like "MAROW" and turned to see Copper pawing at the glass, making a squeaking sound like someone cleaning a windshield at the car wash. They shook their heads, the family shortcut for saying "Copper is acting crazy again," and went back to playing their board game.

Meanwhile, outside in the tree, a barred owl named Bart was about to gobble up one of his favorite evening treats, fresh tree frog, when a weird squeaking sound coming from the door where he had snatched his meal made him pause. Like many owls, his ears were hidden underneath the ring of feathers around his eyes, and one ear was higher than the other to help him pinpoint sounds.

Lopsided Ear Holes

Bart is a barred owl (scientific name *Strix varia*), not to be confused with the similar sounding name barn owl (*Tyto alba*). The circular ring of feathers around his eyes is called a facial disc, which helps direct sound into his ear openings. Since the ears are in different spots on his head, sound arrives at one ear before the other. He knows which direction the sound came from and whether it was high in the trees or close to the ground, and he can move his head to get a precise location. This arrangement of ears is called asymmetrical and it helps him locate prey in the dark.

Asymmetrical ears are great for pinpointing prey, but they make it impossible to find a good-fitting pair of headphones.

Learn more at distractfacts.com/bart.

UNLIKE MOST OWLS, Bart tended to overthink things. It took him a long time to make decisions. He hadn't yet decided what he thought about that, but it was something he wanted to put more thought into.

He carefully placed the unconscious tree frog on the branch and listened to the curious squeaking sound. He stared at the house with his shiny black eyes and zeroed in on an orange tabby cat pawing at the back door. The cat appeared to be saying something, but Bart couldn't make it out.

I wonder if the cat is trying to tell me something, thought Bart. *Maybe this frog belongs to her, or maybe she's trying to warn me about another owl nearby, or maybe the frog is one of those toxic ones mama told me about.* As all these thoughts ran through his mind, Bart was also trying to remember the name of that toxic frog his mama had warned him about. *What kind of frog was it? Pickle frog? Pumpernickel frog? PICKEREL FROG!* Had he caught a pickerel frog? She had told him to look for two rows of square-shaped spots on the frog's back. Bart inspected his catch. There were no square spots, but the frog did have a lot of scratches and scars across its back. As he leaned closer to the frog, the cat began to scratch at the window like she was trying to cut right through it.

She must be trying to tell me that this is a toxic frog, he thought. *I should go check with her just to be sure before I eat it.* Bart fluttered over to the patio and landed with the tree frog gripped in his talons. Then he made a tent with his wings to hide the tree frog from any sneaky dinner thieves hiding in the darkness.

Nothing To See Here!

When an owl bends over and spreads its wings to hide freshly caught prey, it is doing something called "mantling." Other predators might swoop in and steal the owl's food, so it protects the hard-earned meal by making a food tent using its body and wings. Other birds of prey, like hawks and eagles, use the mantling technique as well, especially when they chow down on the ground.

Mantling comes from the word mantle, which is a cloak or covering. The feathers exposed on the bird's back are also called the mantle. This is not to be confused with a mantel, which is the part of a fireplace where some people hang stockings. Owls do not like you to hang stockings on them.

Learn more at distractfacts.com/foodtent.

BART HAD NEVER SPOKEN to a house cat before, and he wasn't sure how well she could hear him inside the house. He decided to shout, just in case. "This frog is toxic, isn't it?" Bart hollered.

The sudden appearance of a screaming owl on her patio caught Copper by surprise. At first, she backpedaled a few steps and considered hiding behind the couch. After a moment to gather her wits, she remembered that she was safe inside her house. Just to make herself feel a little safer, she jumped to the living room windowsill where she could survey the owl from a higher perch.

"Come again?" she sputtered.

"Why should I do that?" questioned Bart. "I just flew over here, and I don't see any reason why I should fly back over there and come back again."

"No, I mean I didn't understand what you said about the frog."

"You're trying to tell me this frog is toxic, right? Is it one of those pickerel frogs?"

"I don't know anything about toxic frogs," exclaimed Copper. "I was having a conversation with a creature, currently beneath your wings, when you stole him right off my porch!"

Before Bart could reply, his belly started talking. At least it seemed that way, as a very groggy froggy beneath Bart's wings awoke from his talon-induced nap. "What happened? Why is it so dark?" Riley cried out from beneath Bart's wings.

Bart lifted his wings and it looked as if the owl had hatched a tree frog on Copper's patio. "No offense," he said, "but I was going to eat you until this house cat got my attention. She had me thinking you might be one of those toxic pickerel frogs."

"Nope, just a regular green tree frog," Riley said with a smile as he put a little distance between himself and Bart. He seemed remarkably calm for a frog who had slipped off another animal's dinner plate. "And no offense taken. When I get dinner invitations, they are always lively and spontaneous like yours. I've met a lot of good creatures that way."

Copper did that head-tilting thing again that cats do. "How can you say they're good when they try to eat you?" she asked.

"They're just trying to get a meal for themselves or their kids, the same as all of us out here. It's not like they do it because they are mean. It doesn't work that way for us," explained Riley.

Bart's empty stomach gurgled. This talk of meals had him ready to make his next move, but he wanted one more piece of information before he made up his mind. "If you aren't a toxic pickerel frog, how come these creatures you've met haven't eaten you?" he wondered.

Riley laughed, and Copper couldn't help but smile because the frog seemed so cheerful. "I know what's on your mind my barred owl friend," said Riley as he turned to face Bart. "Now that you know I'm not toxic, you're trying to decide whether you should finish what you started and gobble me up."

"Pretty much," replied Bart. "Gotta grab a meal when you can, right?" His talons clenched a bit and he leaned closer to the delectable tree frog.

The conversation between a tree frog and an owl on her back porch mesmerized Copper as she watched from the windowsill. Despite her excitement, Copper still had to fight off a brief bout of distractitis. She wasn't sure why, but she had a strong urge to go lay in the middle of her humans' board game. With a waggle of her head, Copper refocused on the tense standoff between the creatures on her porch.

Oddly, Riley didn't seem frightened at all. He wasn't even keeping a close eye on Bart. He watched a seed from a maple tree helicopter its way to the ground behind the owl. A couple of leaves see-sawed to earth in the breeze.

Bart noticed Riley watching the trees and turned his head to investigate. He couldn't see or hear anything, but there was something suspicious about the way the frog was acting.

"I noticed you have a bunch of scars on your back when I had you up in the tree. So, how have you kept yourself alive if you've been in the clutches of so many predators?" Bart thought he saw Riley shaking his head at the trees, like he was trying to communicate with something up there. Jerking his head around to check again, Bart still saw nothing there.

"You put more thought into things than the average owl, don't you?" said Riley. "Most owls would have already swallowed me up and moved on."

Bart turned back to the frog. "Yes, that is a weakness of mine, I think. I really like to think through things before I act. I should probably do less thinking."

Riley peered into Bart's inky black eyes, like he was looking for something hidden behind them. "I wouldn't necessarily call that a weakness," he replied. "It means you aren't the same as every other owl. What is your name?"

"What? Uh, my name is Bart." This was new. Bart wasn't used to being asked for his name when talking to his supper. Come to think of it, he wasn't used to talking to his supper at all.

"Pleased to meet you, Bart. As I was saying to Copper before you swooped in for some delicious tree frog, my name is Riley. To answer your question, I guess I've stayed alive this long due to my dashing good looks."

If Copper had been drinking milk, it most certainly would have shot out of her nose as she stifled a laugh. Riley laughed himself, and he could tell Copper and Bart weren't buying that explanation, so he continued. "Well, if it's not the looks, I guess it helps that I know a lot of creatures. Since I was a young frog, I've always liked to help other animals. That has enabled me to get to know a good many folks and I think that's the only way I've survived so long. I couldn't have done it on my own."

"How does knowing lots of animals make any difference?" asked Bart.

"For one thing, you'd be surprised how many times someone was about to make a snack of me and just before I was on my way down the dark road to Stomachsville, the animal would say 'Oh hey, Riley! I didn't realize that was you.' Some of my friends like to say I'm like the mayor because I know so many critters around Charleston."

Copper stretched out across the windowsill and crossed her paws in front of her. "So, what happens when they don't know you, like Bart here?" she asked.

Riley chuckled. "In those cases, I try to hit them with one of my best jokes. I've got a million of them! Nobody can eat someone who just gave them a good laugh."

"Now this I've got to hear," said Bart. He settled back on his feet. "Tell us one of those lifesaving jokes."

"Gladly!" said Riley. He puffed his chest out a little. "Here's one you might like. Why don't owls tell each other knock-knock jokes?"

And that was the moment when Riley learned not to wait for an answer after telling a joke to an owl who thinks too much. For a long while, Bart stared at Riley as he tried to work out a solution to the joke. Riley began to wonder if he'd have to spend the winter hibernating on Copper's patio. Fortunately, Copper could always be counted on to help, even when she wasn't trying to. She watched Bart's strange milky eyelid slide across his eye every time he blinked. Back and forth went the eyelid with each blink. It was spellbinding. Back and forth, back and forth.

Always Useful to Have a Spare Eyelid

That milky eyelid Copper watched is called a nictitating membrane. Barred owls have a top and bottom eyelid, and the nictitating membrane slides across the eye as a third eyelid. It helps to keep the eye clean and provide protection when swooping in for prey. Many birds and other creatures have nictitating membranes, including cats!

Learn more at distractfacts.com/triplelid.

THE HYPNOTIC EFFECT of Bart's blinking worked its magic on Copper. Her eyes closed, and she was off to cat dreamland where scratching posts are on every corner and rivers of wet food flow through the city like the canals of Venice.

And then she fell off the windowsill.

Copper sprang to her feet, looking at her humans and hoping they hadn't noticed her embarrassing moment. Yep, those were clearly "Copper is acting crazy again" headshakes coming her way. She stretched her back to make it look like she had planned it all and then jumped back to the windowsill. "Did I miss anything?" she asked her new patio friends.

"I'm still trying to figure out the solution to Riley's joke," replied Bart.

"Soooo, I'm thinking you are supposed to say something

like 'I don't know, why don't owls tell each other knock-knock jokes?' and then Riley can tell you the joke part."

"It's strange that he would ask a question that he doesn't want me to try to answer, but okay. So, why don't owls tell each other knock-knock jokes, Riley?"

"Because they always get into a fight over who gets to say 'Hooo's There,'" Riley replied with a wide smile across his frog lips.

Bart stared blankly at Riley, like he didn't get the joke, but something in the trees was laughing hysterically and shaking the branches so hard that several more leaves fell into Copper's yard. Bart crouched and prepared for takeoff. "Who is that hiding in the trees?" he cried.

"Don't worry," Riley answered calmly. "That's Big Strig. He's the reason I've managed to escape from the predators who don't know me or who don't appreciate my spectacular jokes."

4

LET'S OWL GET TOGETHER ON THE PATIO

Copper's tail poofed and Bart bolted from the patio as a fierce owl with spooky yellow eyes glided out of the trees. He stretched out huge wings with tips like fingers as he settled onto the patio. This new owl was twice the size of Bart, but unlike the barred owl, the newcomer appeared to have a pair of pointy ears on his head.

"Copper, I'd like to introduce you to Big Strig," said Riley. "He's a great horned owl."

She was unsure what to say, so as she normally did, she went with the first thing that popped into her head. "Nice ears!" Copper blurted. She instantly wished she could suck the words back in.

"Those aren't ears," the big owl replied in a voice like a low rumble of thunder. "They're my tufts. Just feathers that look like ears."

"Oh, right. That makes sense," Copper said, even though it didn't make sense. She noticed a thin line of white feathers across his eyes like angry eyebrows. Copper decided not to ask him about that.

Naming Things Is Hard

The great horned owl is named for the pair of long feather tufts atop its head, but those aren't horns. They are often called ear tufts, but they aren't ears either. Like the barred owl, the ear openings on a great horned owl are hidden beneath the facial disc feathers around its eyes.

The correct term for the feather tufts is plumicorns, but plumicorned owl gives the impression of an owl with a purple unicorn on its head. That would totally ruin the owl's reputation as a powerful predator.

Learn more at distractfacts.com/earhorns.

"STRIG GOES WITH ME EVERYWHERE," said Riley. "He gives me a lift when I travel to headquarters and lends extra muscle in sticky situations." Big Strig clacked his beak and looked down at his powerful, razor-sharp talons. If owls could flex, he was totally flexing.

"He helps you travel to headquarters?" asked Copper. "What's a headquarters?"

"Excellent question," Riley replied. "Big Strig and I are members of a special organization known as the FLOCC. Headquarters is where our leadership team meets, and we're here to take you there tonight, if you'll come."

"Me?" said Copper, stunned. Thinking it might be perfectly normal for frogs to invite cats to a headquarters, Copper decided to play it cool. "What do you need me for? How do you even know who I am?"

"The FLOCC has known about you for a while," explained Riley. "We think you might be the kind of animal we look for: one who would be interested in helping other creatures."

Copper couldn't believe what she was hearing. A mysterious organization of animals knew who she was? And they wanted to talk to her? She was just an ordinary house cat! "The FLOCC sounds intriguing, and I do like the idea of helping other creatures," she said. "But I don't think I would be much help. I stay inside mostly, so I know more about humans than I do other animals."

"As a matter of fact, your connection with humans is one of the reasons we know about you," said Riley. "But that's not why we're here tonight. We think you can help with an emergency situation involving one of our FLOCC members and . . ." Riley stopped and tilted his head to listen as chairs slid across the floor and closet doors slammed inside the house. "What are they doing in there?" he asked.

Just as she started to explain, Copper noticed the frog didn't have any visible ears. He did have a round, flat spot like a tiny cupholder behind his eye. She wondered if the round spot might be an ear, but after her confusion with Big Strig's tufts, she wasn't about to bring up the ear topic again.

Here We Go with the Ears Again

That little cupholder behind Riley's eye is called the tympanum, and that's the spot where a frog does its hearing. The tympanum works like a human's eardrum and sends sound waves to the frog's inner ear.

Most frogs and toads have a tympanum behind the eye, so look for it the next time you see one around. Do NOT try to set your miniature coffee cup in it. The frog will be very annoyed, and you will spill your coffee.

Learn more at distractfacts.com/canyouearme.

"I THINK they're getting ready for sleep," Copper reassured Riley, trying not to stare at the weird ear spot. "The kids always put on special fur suits before they go to their beds. Those things are so soft! I love to knead my claws on them when they leave them on the floor. It looks like the smallest one has her fur on already."

"They put on special fur suits before they go to bed?" Riley's eyes bulged even more than usual. "That's just weird."

"I know, right?" Copper agreed. "Like I said, I don't understand them that well."

"You know a lot more than we do," said Riley. "So, if you are interested in helping us, we'll bust you out of there and get you to headquarters to discuss the mission."

"Bust me out of here? How would you do that?"

Riley gave a nod to Big Strig, who nodded his understanding. "Ram, come on out!" the owl bellowed.

With a sudden clatter of crackling branches, something large stirred in the woods behind Copper's house. She strained to see what was making all the racket. Out of the thicket popped the weirdest looking dog Copper had ever seen. Except, she wasn't entirely convinced that it was a dog.

He was brown, with white spots all along his sides and quite a bit larger than an average dog. But that wasn't what made him so peculiar. He had a scruffy beard hanging below his mouth and a hefty set of horns sticking out of his head. *Weirdest. Dog. Ever.* Copper thought. She sniffed at the window screen to check for a familiar scent from her new visitor. "Ewwwww! What is that smell?" Copper crinkled her nose and squinted her eyes. "Compared to that, my litter box smells sweet and flowery."

"The aroma you are enjoying is probably our friend Ram here," an amused Riley explained.

The funny looking animal stepped forward. "My name is Ram, but that's what I do, not what I am."

"Could you repeat that?" asked Copper. The stench was so bad her eyes watered, and she wondered if her hearing was clogged as well.

"He said his name is Ram, but he always feels like he has to explain. You see, a ram is a male sheep, but he's a goat, not a sheep. We call him Ram because he rams stuff for us," Riley answered, as if he was explaining a basic fact like cats purr or frogs jump.

Ram kneeled on his front legs like he was bowing to Copper. "Pleasure to meet you my feline friend, to be at your service is what I intend." His stink made Copper want to scratch her nose off her face, but his voice was smooth and musical. Each word floated in the air like a strum on a well-tuned guitar.

Copper licked the side of her paw and rubbed it across her face to relieve her watering eyes. She considered holding her breath while she spoke. "Nice to meet you too, Ram," she gagged. "You have an interesting way of speaking."

Ram got back to his feet. "Ever since my days as a kid, talking like this is what I did."

"Yeah, we thought maybe something got rattled in his head

because he enjoys ramming things so much, but he says he's always been this way," added Riley.

At that moment, Copper noticed that Riley was speaking strangely himself, almost like he was trying to move his lips as little as possible. "You'll get used to the rhyming a lot sooner than the smell, I'll go ahead and tell you that." Riley shuddered. "He smells even worse than this in the summertime. I try to keep my mouth closed whenever we hang out. Lucky for Ram though, his missus loves his bouquet."

Hearing this, Ram held his head high and nodded. "My scent is a rose, to my lady's nose."

Funky Cologne

Think of the most disgusting smell you've ever whiffed. Now multiply that smell times infinity. That is the smell of the male goat, which is awful if your math is correct. Mostly produced by scent glands near the horns, those noxious fumes captivate the lady goats. If that doesn't bring the girls around, male goats will also pee on themselves to get the ladies' attention. This is why no one ever wants to share a bus seat with a goat.

Learn more at distractfacts.com/stankygoat.

COPPER COULD ALMOST FEEL Ram's foul odor pressing against her fur as it wafted through the window.

"Auugh! Mama, what stinks so bad?" one of the children cried.

"It's probably Copper's litter box. Mason, you need to change that out before you go to bed," his mama replied.

"Can't Molly do it?" he begged. "Nine-year-olds are perfectly capable of changing a litter box."

"Well, you're twelve and it's your job," Molly hollered from upstairs. "I'm the one who has to scoop up Oscar's presents in the yard!"

While the poop responsibility battle raged behind her, Copper looked over her shoulder to make sure no one was coming to close the window. It always annoyed her when they closed it before they went to sleep. For now, the coast was clear. "How would Ram bust me out?" choked Copper as she turned back to the window. "Does the smell melt the walls?"

"A few hits to that door, and the glass is no more," said the smelly, silky-voiced goat.

Riley grinned. "Other than smelling so good, Ram's specialty is breaking us into and out of places. We only use this method when we don't have time to plan another way. It makes a mess, but it is very effective."

Copper didn't like that idea at all. She remembered how unhappy her humans looked when they cleaned up the broken glass after the Christmas Tree Incident. "We can't do that. I don't want to upset my humans."

"Does that mean you want to come with us, though?" asked Riley.

"No, it means if I *did* come with you, I wouldn't want to do it that way. Do you have other ideas?"

A symphony of cricket trills played in the background as Riley, Big Strig, Ram, and Copper pondered other options.

"What about the dog?" asked a tree with a voice that sounded a lot like Bart the barred owl.

"Bart, you can come back down now," Riley called to the

tree. "Strig won't hurt you." Despite Riley's assurance, Big Strig stretched out his wings to send Bart a subtle message. He'd certainly hurt him if given a reason.

Bart gathered his courage, soared down from the hiding spot in his favorite oak, and landed in the grass a few feet from the patio. Copper wondered if he was keeping a safe distance from Big Strig or staying downwind of Ram's odor.

Don't Hoot So Close to Me

Barred owls have good reason to keep their distance from great horned owls. Barred owls don't have too many predators, but a great horned owl is one predator fierce enough to take down a barred owl and make a meal out of him.

Bart has another reason to dislike great horned owls, but you'll find out about that later.

Learn more at distractfacts.com/owlwars.

"YOU SAID SOMETHING ABOUT A DOG. How do you know a dog lives here?" Riley questioned Bart.

"I've seen him out in the yard a few times," replied Bart.

Copper interrupted with a sudden thought that came into her mind. "Hey, were you thinking about trying to eat him too?"

"Possibly," said Bart as he made eye contact with Big Strig, who gave him an understanding nod. Bart nodded back. Owls gotta eat.

"Fair enough," Riley continued. "How could we use the dog to get Copper out?"

"I've noticed the dog comes in and out of the house on his own," explained Bart. "He has a special door that he opens and closes with his mind power."

Copper erupted with laughter. She laughed so hard she nearly fell from the windowsill again. "Wooo!" she said as she pulled herself together. "Sorry, Bart, I wasn't laughing at you. The thought of Yap having mind power is hysterical."

"His name is Yap?" Riley and the owls asked in unison.

"My humans call him Oscar, but he's Yap to me because he never stops yapping! That dog barks at everything. If a butterfly flew by and pooped on the patio, Yap would be barking as if he saw a dozen cats out there."

"Where is he now?" wondered Big Strig. "I would think our little gathering here would have grabbed his attention."

Copper kicked out a leg for a quick tongue cleaning. "Probably already in one of the kids' beds upstairs. He likes to sleep with them. I suspect he's afraid of the dark."

Riley looked to the sky as if he was working something out in his mind. "What type of dog is he?" he asked.

Briefly pausing her leg scrub, Copper closed an eye and tilted her head like she was trying to slide a memory out of her brain. "I *think* he's a Miniature Schnauzer."

"Bless you!" Riley took a step back from the window. "You were saying he is a miniature what?"

"Huh? No, I wasn't sneezing, I said he is a Miniature Schnauzer."

"Gesundheit!" came the well-mannered response from the tree frog. "I wonder if you might be allergic to your own fur with all that sneezing. Anyway, all I need to know is that he is a miniature whatever. I think we can work with a tiny dog."

Copper decided not to try to explain Yap's breed any further.

"Anyway, that door opens only for him," she informed the group. "But it definitely isn't opened with his mind power. It has something to do with his collar. If he doesn't have it on, the door won't open. When he goes near it with that collar on, it opens right up. Sometimes he walks by and it slides open when he isn't expecting it. Then he runs into the kitchen to hide and barks at the door like it tried to bite him."

"Maybe the collar magnifies his mind power somehow," pondered Bart.

"Guys, if you knew Yap like I know Yap, the mind power thing would not seem likely."

"I trust your judgment," said Riley. "Either way, it sounds

like the dog is the key to getting you out of there. I think I have an idea, but it's time for you to decide. Do you want to help us out?"

Copper stood and swished her tail from side to side. For the first time in her life, she had an opportunity to go on a real adventure. She had two owls and a tree frog on her porch, animals she hadn't even known existed before, and the frog was offering her a chance to meet even more unfathomable creatures. It sounded fantastic!

On the other paw, the world outside her house seemed scary. The outside animals didn't have piles of food in their bowls, and from what she could tell, they were constantly trying to eat each other. It was a lot nicer inside her house where things weren't scary, and she was comfortable and content.

Comfortable and content. She heard Sarge's voice inside her head. "Never be content being content," he had told her.

"Never pass up the chance for a new adventure," she said to herself. "That's what Sarge would have said."

"Daddy, I hear Copper meowing at the window," Mason shouted from upstairs. "Don't forget to close it."

"Yep, I'll get it before I come up," his daddy replied from the kitchen. "I've heard a couple of owls outside tonight. She's probably wanting to get out there and chase them. I think one of them is a great horned owl, though. She wouldn't want to tangle with one of those."

Who's That Hooting?

Owls have very distinctive calls and once you've heard them once or twice, you'll easily be able to identify any

owls you hear at night. When a barred owl like Bart is talking, it sounds something like 'HOO-HOO-HA-HOO, HOO-
HOO-HA-HOOO-ALL' to a human. Go ahead and practice
that a few times so you can perfect it. Sometimes, if you do
a great call and one is nearby, they will answer you.

When a great horned owl like Big Strig talks, humans hear
something more like 'HOO-HA-HOO, HOOOO-HOO!' Try
that one a few times too, but don't forget that frog-calling
and owl-hooting may be frowned upon in the library.

Learn more at distractfacts.com/whohooted.

REALIZING that this was the opportunity for adventure she had
always craved, Copper made up her mind. "Okay, I'm in."

"Alright then, let's get leaping!" Riley turned to the brawny
great horned owl. "Strig, do you remember the method we
used for the Smoky Squirrel Incident?"

"When we rescued the squirrel that fell into a human's fireplace? How could I forget that one? I still find bits of soot in
my feathers from time to time." Big Strig looked Copper over.
"I can lift her, but I'm not sure we can both fit up the chimney."

"I don't think so either," agreed Riley, "but we won't come
out of the chimney. That's just where we're going to go in.
Ram, stay close in the woods in case we need your services."

"In the trees I shall hide, so I won't be spied," the foul-
smelling, sweet-sounding goat answered.

"What about me?" asked Bart. "I want to help."

Riley's smile grew wider than Copper had seen it all night.
"Bart, you don't know how happy I am to hear that from you.

But as much as I hate to say it, I don't think we can get you involved right now because this is a dangerous mission. I will bring your name up to the FLOCC once all of this is over, though."

"I'm used to dealing with danger," Bart muttered as he flew away. "Thanks to guys like your big owl friend, I've dealt with it alone my whole life."

Riley tried to explain further, but Bart was gone. His gaze lingered on the woods where Bart had disappeared and then he turned to the great horned owl. "Well, Strig, let's take a look at the chimney and I'll fill you in on the rest of the plan."

"Wait, what do I need to do?" cried Copper.

"Just be ready when the moment comes!" Riley shouted as he flew off in the careful grip of Big Strig's talons.

Copper tilted her head and tried to watch them as one of her humans closed the window. *What moment?* she thought.

5

WHOOOO NEEDS A KEY WHEN YOU'VE GOT A YAP

Riley and Big Strig settled on the damp, mossy bricks atop Copper's chimney and peered into the darkness below. "I can see a little bit of light down there," said Riley. "We should be able to make it into the house."

"What are you going to do once we get in there?"

"I'm going to try to talk to the dog. Maybe I can convince him to help us out and open his special door."

Big Strig surveyed the roof. "I don't like this one, Riley. After we get in there, I won't have a lot of room to maneuver."

"I know, Strig. I'm hoping I can reason with the dog." Riley glanced up at Big Strig before adding, "If not, I'll need you to step in."

Big Strig rattled his beak and growled. "You want me to disembowel him?"

"What?" said Riley.

"Disembowel, it means I'll yank out his—"

"I know what it means, Strig. No, that won't be necessary."

"Hold on a minute. I'd like to hear more about this disemboweling," echoed a voice up the chimney.

Riley laughed. "I assume it's safe for us to come down now, Copper?"

"Yep. Everyone is upstairs. Yap is sleeping at the end of Mason's bed."

"Who is Mason?" asked Big Strig.

"One of my humans," Copper squinted her eyes and thought for a second before continuing. "At least, I'm pretty sure that's his name because I hear the adult humans saying it to him a lot, especially right before he cleans out my litter box."

"Okay. We're coming down," called Riley.

Riley and Big Strig shimmied and padded down the chimney, dropping into the empty fireplace. As she sniffed the scent of new creatures, Copper backed away. Now that they were in her living room without the barrier of a screen, it was like their wildness had activated senses she hadn't used before. Big Strig noticed Copper had arched her back and that her tail puffed up. He leapt over Riley to stand between the cat and the frog, sliding a foot forward from beneath his feathers. Copper's ears twitched as the owl's sharp talons scraped against the wood floor.

Big Strig's talons intimidated her, but his glowing yellow eyes petrified Copper. His glare had a weight to it, like she could feel him sitting on her shoulders. Fear washed over her, and she couldn't decide what to say or do. The wrong move might cause Big Strig to take the offensive and inflict serious pain. Staring into his eyes, Copper felt time slow down . . . until a tree frog popped up between the tufts on top of Big Strig's head.

"You know, Strig, we have to figure out a way for you to protect me that doesn't involve you sticking your butt in my face."

Big Strig tried to hold back his laughter and shook so hard

that Riley needed maximum sticky-toed grip power to hang on. Copper fought to contain her own laughter, and they all stood whisper-giggling in the middle of the living room.

"So, Copper," Riley said once they all had caught their breath, "that certainly won't be the last time you meet new creatures tonight. Not all of them will be as friendly as Strig. Are you sure you still want to do this?"

The notion of facing something scarier than Big Strig made Copper want to hide behind the couch. "I still want to go," she stammered, "but I can't guarantee there won't be more tail poofing."

"Totally natural!" Riley assured her. "You can't control that any more than I can stop being so handsome." He moved on before anyone could comment. "Can you lead me to your friend Yap? I want to try to have a word with him."

"Sure thing, but make sure you're ready when the moment comes," warned Copper.

"What moment?" said Riley, but Copper was already climbing the stairs. Following the cat, Riley hopped up the stairs two at a time and squatted next to her outside Mason's room. Copper looked back, expecting Big Strig to be on the stairwell. He had vanished.

At the foot of Mason's bed, a small dog snoozed on his back with front paws curled in the air like fuzzy candy canes. His fur was the color of a thundercloud, with a shaggy white Santa Claus beard around his mouth. As he snored, the beard swayed in the breeze, each exhale sounding like a cricket sneezing.

"What does he have wrapped around him?" whispered Riley.

Copper sighed. "I think it's called a 'hoodie'. Humans wear them, but that one was made for a dog."

"Is he being punished for something?"

"No, I think he actually likes it."

"You're pulling my frog leg, right? Why would an animal with perfectly good fur *want* to wear—" Glancing at Copper's walking harness, Riley stopped himself. "Uh, do you have a 'hoodie?'"

"No way!" Copper noticed Riley eyeballing her walking harness. "My humans put this thing on me when they take me outside." Waving a paw at the slumbering schnauzer in his hoodie she added, "I'd almost rather have a bath than wear one of those—" Just thinking about the bathtub caused Copper to cringe. "Well, almost, anyway."

"Ah! That's good to know." A brief awkward silence passed between them as cat and frog sat side-by-side at the threshold to Mason's room, watching the comatose canine. Then, Riley bravely hopped through the doorway to get a closer look. "Does he have the special collar on?" he whispered. "I can't tell."

Copper crept up behind Riley, her pupils wide and her ears perked. "It's there," she said. "I can see the outline of the little box attached to his collar."

"Let me see if I can get his attention," said Riley. He gave a single, soft call, like a grasshopper landing on a piano key.

One of Yap's ears unfolded.

"Excuse me, may I have a word with you?" Riley loudly whispered.

Yap shook his head and sprang to his feet. His oversized ears stood at attention like two Egyptian pyramids constructed atop his noggin. Standing statue-still, he stared at the doorway.

"Hi there, friend, my name is Riley and I was wondering—"

Yap leapt from the bed and charged at Riley, unleashing a flurry of barks so loud and high-pitched that every piece of glass from Charleston to San Francisco could have been shattered. For a split second, Riley wished he had hands so that he could put them over his ear spots. Then his instincts took over. Riley leapfrogged over Copper and led her in a race down the stairs as Yap gave chase. Lights flicked on as grown-ups and kids awoke to the sounds of Yap's ear-piercing barks and the pounding of cat, frog, and dog feet as all three creatures dashed down the stairs.

It was a photo finish in the inaugural Copper's House Stair Sprint as the participants crossed the finish line at the bottom of the stairs. Copper might have won by a whisker, but Riley was airborne, so it was difficult to tell who got there first.

"Split up!" commanded the booming voice of Big Strig from somewhere in the shadows of the kitchen. Copper rounded the kitchen island and doubled back toward the living room. Riley speed-hopped toward the crack under the pantry door. Yap ignored Copper and sprinted after the fleeing tree frog. Nipping at Riley's trailing leg, the schnauzer slammed into the pantry at maximum speed as the tree frog scampered safely under the door. Yap waggled his head and immediately resumed his berserk barking at the pantry. He pawed at the base of the door like he was trying to dig up the world's largest bone, repeatedly sticking his round, black nose underneath. Now safely tucked away in the dimly lit pantry, Riley watched as the big, wet gumdrop kept appearing beneath the door.

Careening down the stairs like a runaway freight train, Copper's half-dazed humans ran to investigate Yap's frenzied barking. They had each grabbed a weapon for personal defense. Mama had a pillow locked and loaded. Mason was on deck with a foam baseball bat propped on his shoulder. Molly had a two-handed grip on her butterfly net like a sword-wielding Samurai warrior.

Daddy had a plunger.

Their best hope to catch an intruder would be to put the

butterfly net over the villain's head and whack him with the pillow and foam bat while Daddy unclogged the toilet.

"Humans are on the way!" yelled Big Strig over Yap's yapping.

"Get Copper out! I'm safe in here for the moment!" Riley shouted from the pantry.

Copper stood bewildered by the front door. "How are we supposed to do that?" she hollered.

"Use the dog!" said Riley.

"He won't come to the door!" cried Copper, but Big Strig knew what he had to do. Swooping down from the kitchen cabinets with talons out, the owl locked his eyes on Yap's hooded sweatshirt.

The clamor of frog calling, cat yowling, owl hooting, and Yap yapping in the living room froze Daddy at the base of the stairs, but evidently his brake lights weren't working. Mama slammed into him, causing Daddy to tumble onto the living room floor. With her pillow providing a convenient soft landing, Mama fell on his back. Next came the kids, like two bowling balls crashing into Mama and Daddy pins.

The four-human pileup at the foot of the stairs caused Yap to turn just in time to see a pair of huge wings, eight black talons, and two yellow eyes appear out of nowhere. The talons dug into his sweatshirt and before he could bark once more, Yap was a flying dog.

"Wait by the door!" Big Strig huffed to Copper as he airlifted the dog across the kitchen with a firm grip on the sweatshirt.

"An owl has Oscar!" Daddy cried as he scrambled to his feet. The cup-shaped rubber piece on the plunger had popped off when he fell. Hoping to force the owl to drop the dog, he picked up the rubber piece and hurled it at Big Strig.

Big Strig dipped below the unidentified flying plunging object (UFPO) and hovered above the doggie door. As Yap whimpered and struggled to escape from the sweatshirt, a strange silence fell over the rest of the house. Everyone stopped at the whirring sound of Yap's doggie door sliding open. The collar had done its job.

"Go!" Big Strig boomed as the sweatshirt began to rip in his talons. Copper panicked and started to run in the wrong direction. "Out—the—door!" Big Strig grunted through his clenched beak.

Copper turned and raced toward the doggie door. In her haste, she failed to notice the plunger cup lying in front of the doormat and stepped into the cup at a full sprint. Her foot wedged into the hole in the plunger cup and her momentum sent her flying head over paws right into Big Strig. Yap's sweatshirt ripped apart, and as the dog ran for cover, a ball of cat, owl, and plunger cup tumbled through the open doggie door into the night air. The door hummed shut behind them.

Yap ran for the protection of his humans, but Daddy leapt over him as he sprinted for the door. When he yanked the door open, to his surprise, he found a goat standing on his porch.

"Good evening, my good man, why is that stick in your hand?" questioned Ram. Of course, that's not what Daddy heard. He heard something more like "Meh-eh-eh-ehhhh!"

"Goaaaaaaat!!!" Daddy shrieked in a voice a few octaves higher than normal. He slammed the door in Ram's face and turned to see his family standing there, looking very confused.

"Did you say goat?" Mama asked.

Meanwhile, outside the house, Ram was trying to stomp the plunger cup with his hoof to help Copper free her foot. Big Strig was panting as he paced back and forth talking to himself. "I've got to get Riley," he said. "He's trapped in there and has no way out."

"Can you not try again, the way you went in?" asked Ram.

Big Strig flailed his wings as he looked up at the chimney. "They're all stirred up in there. They'll see me coming. I'd have to swoop in, signal Riley, get him out in the open where I could grab him, and then fly back up the chimney without either one of us getting caught. Without the element of surprise, I don't know if we can pull that off. You may have to ram your way in."

"Don't do that," interrupted Copper. She was trying to lick at her stuck paw, but it was tough to open her mouth so close to Ram's stink. She muttered through closed teeth, "I don't want anyone to get hurt."

"Riley's gonna get more than hurt if we don't get him out of there," Big Strig snarled. "Did you see how that crazy dog was going after him?"

"I got the impression that Riley was pretty resourceful at getting out of tight situations," said Copper. "Can't we give him a little time to see if he can work it out on his own?"

"There is no doubt Riley can find a way out," Ram agreed.

"I owe that frog my life," said Big Strig. "I'd be dead at the claws of my own kind if not for him. I can't just sit here and hope he gets out on his own."

Focusing on the task at hand, Ram placed both of his front hooves on the plunger cup. "Now let us see if you can pull your foot free," he said.

Copper strained to pull her paw from the hole, but she couldn't get it to budge. "Maybe if we—" she started, but a most annoying sound inside the house interrupted her. Yap was barking again. Big Strig rocketed toward the chimney.

With the big owl out of the house, Yap had regained enough courage to resume his hunt for the tiny tree frog. He was back at the pantry door barking and pawing at it like a mad dog. Copper's humans gathered around the door. They had no idea what was in there, but they'd already encountered an owl in the house and a goat on their porch, so anything was possible. With everyone's weapons at the ready, Daddy turned the knob and eased the door open, hinges creaking. Yap stopped barking and backed up a couple of steps as a shaft of light from the kitchen spread across the pantry, revealing a solitary green tree frog sitting on the floor next to a box of kitty treats.

"Hi folks!" Riley said in his usual cheery tone. Naturally, Copper's humans didn't hear that. Instead, they heard this:

"Meeeeep!"

And then, Yap charged with as loud and annoying a bark as he could muster.

Riley expected the charge and leapt as Yap pounced, bouncing off the dog's head and past his tail like he was on a froggy doggy obstacle course. Molly's frog-catching instincts kicked in. Swinging her butterfly net at the leaping amphibian, she missed her target, capturing her brother's head instead. Mason swung around wildly with foam bat in hand, making a direct hit with Daddy's midsection.

Down went Daddy.

Later, the family debated whether Mama was laughing at that moment or not. Only Mama could tell you that for sure.

Riley had escaped the humans, but Yap had not given up. While the frog leapt across the kitchen floor with no idea where to go, the house echoed with the shrill yapping of the dog in hot pursuit. The loose scrap of his torn hoodie flapped at his side as he raced after the frog. Knowing he couldn't outrun the dog, Riley had an unwise idea flash into his mind. He decided to stop and try to reason with Yap again. Riley skidded to a halt, then turned to face the charging canine.

"Hey, I love your hoodie," Riley exclaimed. "Do you know if they make that in frog size?"

Yap opened his jaws and leapt at the frog, only to come up with a mouthful of air. Once again, an owl had materialized in the living room, grabbing the frog before Yap could clamp down.

"Daddy, the owl is back, and he has the frog!" shrieked Molly.

"Unnnngh huh," her daddy groaned from his fetal position on the floor.

Shooting into the fireplace, the owl began to ascend the chimney with Riley in his talons. "Thanks for saving me, Strig," said the frog as he tried to catch his breath.

"I'm on my way down!" Big Strig's voice boomed from the top of the chimney.

Riley's heart skipped a beat. "What? Then who's carrying

me?"

Atop the chimney, Big Strig stepped aside as Bart the barred owl emerged with a very grateful tree frog clutched in his claws.

"How did you get in there?" asked the stunned great horned owl.

"I snuck down the chimney right after you and Riley went in," replied Bart. "You two were talking to Copper and I hid on that shelf above the fireplace."

Big Strig tilted his head, trying to recall the layout of the house. "I thought those were statues!"

"One of them was," said Bart. "I guess those humans like owls. Anyway, once all the pandemonium began, I didn't know what to do, so I just froze there. But I knew I had to help when the dog was about to chomp on Riley."

"I thank you very much for saving me, Bart," said Riley. "You have shown us a lot about your heart tonight."

Big Strig cleared his throat. "I hate to break up the huggy moment here, but we've got a problem. Copper has something stuck on her foot, she can't walk with it on there, and we need to get back to headquarters. Should we leave her here and drop this whole idea?"

Riley took a deep breath. "No, it's time for the FLOCC to test this idea. We've been talking about it for over a year and she's out of the house now. Do you think you can carry her?"

Big Strig stretched out one wing, and then the other. "I've already warmed up with some miniature dog lifts. I guess a small cat should be no problem."

"I knew you had it in you, Strig." Riley turned from the great horned owl to the barred owl. "Bart, that means my usual ride is booked. Would you be interested in giving me a lift? It isn't far from here."

This was one of the few times in Bart's life when he didn't need to put a whole lot of thought into his decision. He excitedly replied, "Go with you to FLOCC headquarters and help out on a mission? You don't have to ask me twice!"

"I don't know that you'll be allowed on the mission," said Riley, "but we can talk about that when we get there. Let's get leaping!"

Big Strig whooshed from the chimney, swooped into the yard, and yanked Copper up by the metal ring on her purple walking harness. He struggled to gain altitude and pumped his wings with all his might to clear the treetops. Copper wanted to ask if Riley was okay, but the shock of being a flying cat left her speechless. Her question was answered when Bart soared alongside with Riley riding in his talons.

On the lonely road just beyond Copper's house, a young man named Kyle was driving his flatbed tow truck home from a late-night traffic accident. Something appeared in his side mirror and he braked the truck hard. He could have sworn that he saw two owls fly across the road behind him, and that one was carrying a frog with its legs dangling in the air. Was the other owl carrying a cat with a plunger cup on its leg? That couldn't be right.

Switching off the strobing yellow lights on his truck, Kyle stepped out onto the highway. He studied the trees flanking both sides of the road and listened to the chorus of frogs and crickets, but there was no sight or sound of any owls.

Kyle shrugged his shoulders and slid his lanky frame back into the truck. Even if his eyes weren't playing tricks on him and he had truly seen two owls carrying a cat and a frog, it wasn't anywhere near the strangest thing he had seen animals do.

6

THE CROWS ON THE BUS GO CAW CAW CAW

Copper didn't know much about flying. Actually, she didn't know anything about flying, but she had a sneaking suspicion that her feet should not be smashing into treetops. A wake of falling leaves trailed behind them as Big Strig struggled to keep her aloft. The plunger cup on her foot was a bulldozer blasting through thin branches. "Do you think you could get a little higher?" asked the frightened feline.

Big Strig dropped a tad lower.

"O . . . kay . . . I . . . get . . . the . . . point," Copper stammered as pine needles smacked her in the face. "You . . . are . . . doing . . . the . . . best . . . you . . . can!" She winced as she prepared for a pinecone to embed itself in one of her nostrils but was relieved when Big Strig returned to his previous altitude. Copper decided not to offer any more flying advice to the pilot.

"Hang in there, Copper, it's just over this last batch of trees," Riley yelled from his comfy seat in Bart's claws.

"Hanging in here is pretty much all I can do at this point!" shouted Copper.

The last of the trees disappeared and a wide clearing

emerged, littered with mangled cars and ancient rust buckets. "Okay, Strig, go ahead and drop her!" Riley hollered.

"No, wait, what!!!!?" shrieked Copper.

"Kidding, Copper, kidding!" yelled Riley.

"Real funny, frog!" Copper shouted back. "Now I'm down to only eight lives!"

Big Strig dove toward a dusty patch of weeds at the center of the junkyard. As the wind roared in her face, Copper's ears folded back. She felt like she might toss the kibble she'd had for supper. "Shouldn't we be slowing down now?" she cried. As Big Strig opened his broad wings like a parachute, every muscle in Copper's body tensed and she closed her eyes. She felt a lurch as the owl slammed on the brakes and released her from his talons. A tiny dust cloud formed as Copper tumbled across the dirt like a shirt in a dryer, coming to a stop against the dry-rotted wheel of a rusty pickup truck.

"Owww," moaned Copper. "I think I hit my nose with this thing on my foot." She licked a paw and rubbed it against her sore nose, then switched to licking at the dust that covered her from head to tail. Pain management must always take a backseat to personal grooming.

Big Strig landed on the truck and watched as Bart, with Riley in his talons, swung over the clearing. "Just set me down right there next to Strig," said Riley, but Bart swooped down to the roof of an antique ice cream truck across the clearing from Big Strig and dropped Riley safely there instead. "That will work, Bart, thanks for the smooth ride," said the tree frog. He expected the barred owl to land behind him. Bart was not there.

Oh no, this isn't going to be good, thought Riley.

"Bart, you need to come down here right away!" he yelled. "You aren't safe circling around up there!"

I need to get a good look at this place, thought Bart. *This could be some sort of trap. Especially with that great horned owl involved.* He looped above Riley and scanned the trees surrounding the junkyard. Hovering with his beak hanging open, Bart watched as hundreds of crows streamed from every corner of the junkyard, forming a monstrous black cloud that swirled around him like a whirlpool. The army of crows cawed as one, blaring an alarm that thundered across the junkyard.

Swarming Bart, the crows dive-bombed and swiped at him from every direction. He rocketed toward the far end of the junkyard, wings burning as he flapped and thrashed, desperate to outrun the relentless birds. As he neared the edge of the clearing, another legion of crows burst from the trees. Plunging toward a school bus sitting on its axles, Bart darted into one of the window openings. Many of the crows broke from the mob and landed on top of the bus, while others swept in through the open windows. The thump of birds hitting roof and incessant cawing blended into a buzz that echoed in Bart's skull. Clicking his beak and flailing his wings at the unyielding birds, he perched atop a ragged bus seat that had clumps of foam spilling out of it.

Don't Mess with the Mob

When a potential predator like an owl or another bird of prey threatens their territory, crows will gather and swarm the invader. They will dive-bomb the bird, cawing and pecking at the predator until it surrenders and flees the area. Other birds also use mobbing for defense, and sometimes crows are victims of mobbing attacks by birds that consider the crow a predator.

If you want to know what crow mobbing sounds like, you'll
need to get at least one other person to join you. Once you
have your team assembled, keep yelling "caw-caw-caw"
as fast and as loud as you can. It's even more fun if you run
around, flapping your arms like a bird. Please note that you
won't be getting a Christmas card from the librarian if you
do any of that inside the library.

Learn more at distractfacts.com/crowsquad.

COPPER WATCHED in horror as the faded-orange school bus at
the edge of the field turned black as crow after crow settled on
it. The deafening roar of their caws hurt her ears, and she was
used to hearing Yap. While her instincts told her to run and
hide, Copper also felt a powerful urge to help her new friend,
Bart. Neither one of those actions was going to be possible
though, with that plunger cup stuck on her foot. Wondering

what she had gotten herself into, she yowled in fear and frustration.

Riley dashed down the mildewed awning of the ice cream truck where Bart had dropped him and flopped onto the metal counter below. "Brock! Harriet! It's me, Riley!" he shouted into the shadowy truck. "You've got to call them off! That owl is with us!" Riley ducked as two large American crows shot out of the ice cream truck like feathered fighter jets. As they approached the swarm of crows blanketing the bus, the smaller of the pair gave a series of loud rattles which stood out against the frenzied cawing of the mob.

Within seconds, the crow horde cleared the bus and streamed back into the trees encircling the junkyard, leaving only the two shiny-black crows from the ice cream truck. They flew inside and perched on the oversized steering wheel. "You can come out now," the larger of the two crows said to the seemingly empty bus. "Riley says you're with him, so you're safe. At least, for now."

"Don't pay any attention to my surly friend here," the smaller crow said as she swung a scolding wing at her companion. "Come on out. We all need to talk."

Bart had hunkered down on a seat at the rear of the bus. He wasn't in any hurry to step out. He closed his eyes and soaked in the silence that had fallen on the bus. Horrible memories of the last time he had been so terrified flooded his mind.

"Okay," the smaller crow said. "I can understand if you don't want to come right now. We'll be back over there with Riley and Big Strig when you are ready." She turned to her partner. "Let's go, Brock."

Brock didn't budge. He eyed the aisle of the quiet school bus. "Harriet, I think I know where the owl is," he said in a loud whisper.

"Yes, Brock. I have no doubt that you do, but we're going to let the owl come out on his own terms," she loud-whispered back. Harriet then flew out of the driver's window. But Brock lingered on the steering wheel, his glossy brown eyes fixed on one of the seats that happened to have a small white feather striped with brown bars lying underneath it.

"Leave the owl be!" Harriet screeched from outside the bus.

"Coming, dear!" replied Brock, giving an extra loud AWWWK before flying out of the window. Harriet and Brock returned to the ice cream truck and landed on the window counter next to Riley.

"Is he okay?" questioned Riley.

"I think so," Harriet replied. "He's hiding on the bus. Probably more scared than anything."

"Why is he here?" asked Brock. "We're already taking a big risk with the house cat, and now you show up with an owl we've never seen before."

"I'm sorry about that," said Riley, "but we ran into some . . . complications getting Copper out."

All three looked down at Copper, who was leaning against the rusty pickup while Big Strig attempted to pry the plunger cup off her paw. Now that the chaos had settled in the junkyard, Copper had also begun the urgent task of grooming her grubby fur. She stopped at the mention of her name.

"Uh, hi there!" she said with the best smile she could muster.

"Hi," said Harriet. "What is that on your foot?"

"Oh, yeah . . . that. It's kind of a long story." Copper suddenly realized how awkward she looked and nervously licked at the plunger cup. "It's some kind of tool my humans stick in their toilet."

"Did it occur to you that you are licking something they stick in their toilet?" asked Brock.

Copper stopped mid-lick and Big Strig, who was pecking at the plunger cup, trying to free Copper's foot, took a couple steps back from his pecking.

"This moment will never be mentioned to anyone else," Big Strig commanded. "Do we all understand?"

"You mean the moment where your beak touched the humans' toilet tool?" yelled one of the trees at the edge of the field.

Harriet threw her head back and busted out with laughter. Shortly after, the junkyard was showered with the raspy laughs of a thousand crows hidden in the trees. Big Strig flew to the top of the ice cream truck and twisted his head in every direction. The angry gaze of the fearsome owl slowly silenced each section of the woods. Once there was quiet, Big Strig turned his attention to the talking tree.

"I see you found your nerve again, Bart," Big Strig jeered. "Why don't you come down here and let's have a chat?"

Bart shuffled to a different tree and considered how much more he should press his luck. The smart thing to do was to fly away and forget the night had ever happened although it was kind of fun to annoy the burly great horned owl. "I'll come down there, but I hope you don't mind if I keep my distance from you."

"Are you scared of little ole me?" Big Strig boasted while puffing out his feathers.

"No, human toilet breath makes me gag a little," Bart replied.

Rollicking laughter rippled across the field, making a thousand crows sound like two thousand crows. Big Strig had no chance of settling them down again, but the slight smirk on his face hinted that even he had enjoyed the joke. He would never admit it, though. Big Strig patiently listened as the laughter continued for what seemed like minutes, until the crows at one end of the field abruptly stopped laughing. Instead, they began shouting alarm calls again, calls that washed like waves across the junkyard, while the crows themselves stayed hidden in the trees.

"Must be someone we know," said Brock.

They all stared in the direction where the alarm calls had started. Copper's eyes nearly popped out of her head when she saw a black tomcat emerge from behind a wood-paneled station wagon. He had green eyes and a small, lightbulb-shaped patch of white on his chest.

7

NEVER STICK YOUR NOSE IN A TAILPIPE

"Sarge!" Copper squealed as she leapt up to greet him. Forgetting that she had the plunger cup attached to her foot, Copper immediately toppled over. Luckily, Big Strig's pecking had loosened the plunger's grip, and it launched off her foot toward the ice cream truck, scattering all the animals gathered there before spinning safely to a stop below the counter. Copper rolled back to her feet, rushed to Sarge, and gave him the biggest headbutt possible without breaking his nose.

"It's good to see you, little one," Sarge responded with a great big smile on his face.

"You wouldn't call her little if you tried flying her over those trees," said Big Strig as he landed next to them.

"Ha! I doubt it was much trouble for you, old friend," replied Sarge.

"Wait a minute, you two know each other?" asked Copper.

"For many years now," said Sarge. "He's never taken me flying during all that time, though. You must be extra special."

"Trust me, it isn't nearly as much fun as it sounds," said

Copper. "I've missed you, Sarge. My humans named me Copper! I wanted to tell you at the shelter, but you were gone. What happened that night? Where did you go?"

"Ram had to bust me out of there for an emergency mission. I felt terrible about that. Not only did it make a big mess for the shelter workers, but I didn't get to say goodbye to you. But I had a feeling I might see you again."

"So, you know Ram as well? Are you part of the FLOCC?"

"He's one of the oldest members, in more ways than one," Riley chimed in as he and the two crows joined the trio.

Sarge laughed. "I might be old, but Brock and Harriet started the Charleston squad, so they've got me beat there."

"Charleston squad? Are there other FLOCC squads?" asked Copper.

"There are FLOCC squads all over the world," said Harriet.

"Yes, and as the leaders of this squad we need to get moving—"

"Brock, don't make Copper think we're the only leaders," Harriet interrupted. "We may have founded this squad, but we are only a part of the leadership team. Just because we were first doesn't mean we are more important."

"I know, Harriet. I'm just a little anxious to get on with our business," replied Brock. "Lots of weird things going on around here lately."

"Always the worrier, aren't you?" She prodded her beak into the feathers at the back of his neck.

Let Me Get That Fly for You

Crows use their beaks to get at those itchy spots their mates can't quite reach. They do this to help with grooming and removing mites, flies, and other annoying things. This behavior is called allopreening.

Some experts believe allopreening is also a way crows show affection. Because nothing says I love you like, "I just ate a fly off your back."

Learn more at distractfacts.com/flypicking.

"SPEAKING OF WEIRD THINGS," said Sarge, "I heard a big commotion over here as I was coming through the woods. It almost sounded like all the sentries were laughing at something. What was that all about?"

"Oh, that," Big Strig quickly answered. "You probably heard them alerting us to your approach."

"It was before that," countered Sarge. "I'm pretty sure it was thunderous laughter."

"Nah, you must have heard something else," said Big Strig. "Those old ears might not be working as well as they once did."

"No, it was laughter," shouted yet another of the trees at the edge of the field. "Everyone was laughing after Big Strig smooched the human toilet tool."

"Who's the talking tree?" shouted Sarge over the din of a thousand crows, all laughing once again.

"That would be Bart, a barred owl who helped us out of a jam tonight at Copper's house," answered Riley. "He also seems to enjoy poking fun at Big Strig."

Big Strig shot off toward the tree where Bart had made his most recent wisecrack. Taking flight as Big Strig approached,

Bart swooped down to the gathering of animals at the center of the junkyard.

"Welcome to the party, Bart," said Harriet. "I'm Harriet, this is Brock, and over there—"

"Nice to meet you, Harriet," Bart interrupted as Big Strig swept in behind him. Bart shuffled around Riley, using the tiny tree frog as a shield. "I didn't realize such a big, tough owl would be so sensitive."

"We'll see who's sensitive when I get my claws on your neck," Big Strig replied as he lunged toward Bart.

They danced a circle around Riley until Brock's patience ran out. "That's enough!" exclaimed the surly crow. "We are wasting valuable time. Sarge needs to know what's going on. If we're going to try this crazy mission, we need to get moving. Benny could lose everything tonight if we don't figure out how to help him."

"Who's Benny?" coughed Copper, as the cloud of dust stirred up by the two-owl tango settled on her nose.

"Benny is a black-crowned night heron and a member of the FLOCC," answered Sarge. "Some creature has been taking Benny's chicks, but I thought Riley and Big Strig were already working to solve that mystery. What's happened?"

"Strig and I were there to help last night and things . . . didn't go too well," said Riley. "Another night heron's chick was taken, and we have no idea who, or what is doing it. Benny only has one chick left."

"That's terrible!" cried Sarge. "Is his colony still together?"

"A few of the herons left the colony after they got word that another chick was taken," said Harriet.

"That colony has existed longer than any of us have been alive," Brock added. "I'm afraid one more incident will cause the rest of the birds to abandon it forever."

Riley noticed an intense look on Bart's face. He had seen that same look earlier during an awkward knock-knock joke session. The barred owl was thinking about something. "Something on your mind, Bart?" Riley asked.

"There is always something on my mind," replied Bart.

"He's probably trying to think of another wisecrack at my expense," Big Strig grumbled.

"No, for some reason, cracking on you is something that comes to me naturally. I don't even have to think about it. It's like it *flushes* out of my brain whenever I *plunge* into a conversation with you."

"Yeah, yeah, I'm sure it does," mumbled Big Strig. For some reason, he felt a strong desire to wipe a wing across his beak while the rest of the group snickered. "What *is* on your mind then?"

"Why are you all concerned about some other bird's kids and his colony?"

Brock flicked his tail in frustration and turned to Riley. "That question proves he shouldn't be here. We don't know anything about this owl. A FLOCC candidate wouldn't be confused about the reason for helping others."

"I know how cautious you are about new creatures in our group," Riley reassured Brock. "And I know you have plenty of reason to be wary, but I wouldn't have allowed Bart to come here if I hadn't seen something in him."

"I'm not sure you've had enough time to make a reasonable judgement," said Brock.

"Maybe not, but I also didn't have much choice, the way things went at Copper's house. Bart helped us, and he had no selfish reason to do so. It's precisely the kind of thing we look for in new FLOCC members."

"It's the *first* thing we look for, as you well know," insisted

Brock. "How do we know he isn't involved in the disappearance of Benny's children? Why was he hanging around Copper's house the same night you and Big Strig visited?"

"Because I live there," said Bart. He crossed his wings across his chest. "I've been in those woods since the day I lost my mom and dad." His words hung in the air like a cloud over the odd company of animals in the shadowy junkyard.

"I'm sorry you lost your parents," said Harriet. "How did it happen?"

Bart drew in a breath and stared into Harriet's coffee-colored eyes like he was looking for his own reflection. "I've never talked about it. There hasn't been anyone to tell it to anyway."

"And, I'm thinking now is probably not the best time to talk about it," added Brock before anyone else could chime in. "We really don't have the ti—"

Brock ducked as Harriet swiped a wing at him. "I'm willing to listen, if you want to share your story with us, Bart," she said. "It would give us a chance to get to know you."

Bart looked around the group. Big Strig and Brock stood motionless. Copper, Sarge, and Riley all nodded, showing their support.

"I was the only egg Mama laid last year," he began. "A one-egg year is rare, so I got a lot of attention from her and Dad. Early on, he would bring her food and she would feed it to me. Later, they both started to hunt and bring me stuff. Even after I fledged and could leave the nest to hunt on my own, they would still bring me food sometimes. Mama said they were showing me new hunting skills, but I think they liked spoiling me a little."

Bart hesitated, swallowed hard and turned his gaze to Big Strig.

"One night, Dad went out to hunt. While he was gone, Mama wanted to show me a fun way to catch fish. I watched from a branch next to our tree hollow as she dropped into the nearby stream and plucked out a fish. Then as she flew back to me, she was attacked by a great horned owl, just like him."

Big Strig blinked slowly but said nothing.

"I don't know if that owl was after her or maybe he wanted the fish and Mama got in the way," Bart continued. "He carried her off into the woods in his talons as she cried out for Dad. I froze there on the branch, trying to think of what to do." Bart began to sob and struggled to get his words out.

"It's okay, Bart," Harriet comforted. "You were a youngster. You weren't ready for something like that. You certainly wouldn't have been a match for a great horned owl."

"Maybe not," Bart spluttered, "but my dad needed my help. He had heard Mama crying out and came roaring in from his hunt. As he flew by, he screamed that there were multiple birds attacking her and told me to take off and join the fight. I tried to follow him. I wasn't much of a flyer yet, and I lost sight of him. I heard horrible sounds of screeching birds fighting in the forest ahead, and then another great horned owl appeared behind me."

Riley and Big Strig exchanged glances. There was something about Bart's story that sounded very familiar. Riley inched over to Harriet and whispered something into the feathers behind her eye.

"I panicked," Bart continued. "I stopped trying to follow Dad and I veered off, flapping as hard as I could and swerving in and out of the trees. I went as far as I had the strength to fly. It probably wasn't even that far but it felt like it at the time. I crossed over several creeks, human nesting places, and stretches of woods until my wings were burning and I got so tired I had to stop. Looking down, I found a small patch of forest, so I climbed into an old abandoned tree hollow and tried to make myself disappear. The sun was high in the sky the next day before I came out of that hollow."

"Did you try to go back?" asked Brock.

"I had no idea how to get back," snapped Bart. "I had been so scared, I didn't think about paying attention to where I was flying." He continued to glower at Big Strig. "Besides, it was no longer safe there anyway. It had become great horned owl territory, and as Harriet said, barred owls aren't likely to win a battle with great horned owls. My mom and dad learned that the hard way."

"Bart, I'm sorry that you lost your parents," said Brock. "But don't be too hard on yourself. Not only were you just a kid, but you also had to do whatever you could to survive. It's all about survival out here in the wild. You did what any creature would have done in your position, right?"

Bart bowed his head and shuffled the dust with his toes. "I guess so. I tried telling myself that to get through all the many lonely nights afterward." The barred owl sighed. "Every creature for itself."

"But there are certain creatures who are different, as I suspect you already know," said Riley. "Why did you come to help us when we were getting Copper out of her house? Why did you save me from the dog? None of that mattered for your own survival."

"I don't know why I tried to help," answered Bart. "There is a feeling I get sometimes. I've never been able to explain it. It's like I think more than other owls I've seen. Like I'm always trying to figure out—"

"What choice to make?" interrupted Harriet.

"I don't understand what you mean," said Bart.

"Choosing is what makes a FLOCC member, Bart," explained Riley. "There are special creatures in the world who can pick what to do in any situation. They are unlike most creatures, who don't have the ability to choose and only do what comes naturally for survival."

"Are you saying I might have that choosing ability?" asked Bart.

"That's too much for us to sort out tonight," said Brock. "We appreciate your help getting Copper here, but we're in a desperate situation. We've got to use her for a mission. Now."

Copper stood and inched closer to Bart. "If it makes you feel any better, I understand how you feel. I never knew my parents. All my memories begin when I was a kitten at the animal shelter."

Bart studied Copper's face, and after what felt like several minutes to the friendly feline, he broke the awkward silence. "That does make me feel better. I mean . . . not the part about you not knowing your mom and dad, but us having something in common."

Copper smiled and then she began to sniff the air a little. Her eyes started to tear up and Bart thought she might be getting emotional. But instead, Copper's smile vanished from sight as she exclaimed, "Ugh! Is anyone else noticing this? This place just got seriously stinky."

Bart, Big Strig, Brock, and Harriet seemed confused by Copper's comment, but Sarge looked as if he were about to throw up while Riley puffed out his cheeks, holding his breath. Just then, a voice like that of an angel proclaimed, "Sorry I'm late, got stuck in the gate," as a goat that smelled like a fully loaded garbage can appeared from behind the ice cream truck.

"Hey there, Ram!" Harriet called as she flew over and landed between his horns. She pecked him softly on the head.

"You're right on time as usual. We're about to tell Copper why we need her tonight."

Scrumptious Skunks for Supper

Many birds don't have a great sense of smell, and sometimes their meal choices confirm it. Crows don't mind eating a little carrion, which is the rotting flesh of another animal who has already met its end.

Great horned owls munch on a little carrion too, but they take smelly refreshments to another level. They love to eat skunks. There aren't many other predators who will snack on those stripy sprayers of stinky stuff. Any animal that can eat a skunk will have no problem sharing a bus seat with a funky goat.

Learn more at distractfacts.com/stinkysnacks.

COPPER HAD STUCK her face in the tailpipe of the pickup truck, hoping to get relief from Ram's funk. She tried to pull her nose out. Her muzzle wouldn't budge. "I uh, might need a little help over here," she pleaded as she wriggled her rear end trying to free her face.

Brock shook his head at the sight of Copper's backside wiggling around at the end of the tailpipe. Harriet laughed hysterically from her perch on Ram's head. Big Strig flapped over to the pickup truck to lend some muscle, but the stinky goat had his own idea to solve the problem.

"I'll get her free, leave it to me," said Ram.

Heeding Ram's warning, Sarge backed away from the truck. All the other animals followed his lead. They had seen Ram work his magic before.

"What are you going to do?" Copper asked in a nervous, tailpipe-muffled voice.

Ram didn't answer. He had retreated to the opposite side of the little clearing. He lowered his head and launched toward the pickup truck like a cheetah chasing a gazelle. As Copper was straining against the tailpipe and pawing at it to free herself, she heard goat hooves thumping on the dusty earth. Out of the corner of her eye, she saw a set of horns appear, giving her a split-second to brace herself before . . .

THWUMP! Ram smashed into the side of the decrepit pickup truck. It shuddered, and the flattened rear tire lifted off the ground. As the truck plopped back to its longtime resting place, the rusty tailpipe broke loose. Copper tumbled backwards into freedom. Well, not total freedom.

"Copper, I think you have a little something stuck to your face," Riley joked as Big Strig's whole body quivered with silent laughter.

"Thanks for letting me know," said Copper as she got back on her feet. Sounding like she was mumbling through a cardboard tube, she added, "I'd hate to walk around with something on my face and not know it's there. That would be embarrassing."

"Would you like me to point out where it is?" asked Bart. "I'm always happy to help."

"I don't think that will be necessary," Copper replied. "I think I have a pretty good idea of where it is."

"Is it hurting you? Please tell me it isn't hurting you," said Harriet.

"Fortunately, it doesn't hurt," replied Copper. "Does it look bad?"

"It looks like you have a bill. Sort of like a duck laid an egg and out popped a cat," said Riley.

As if someone had tickled them all at once, the whole gang began howling with laughter at the dust-covered orange tabby house cat with a broken piece of tailpipe stuck on her face.

Big Strig was laughing so hard he was bent over like he was trying to touch his toes with his beak. Bart had a wing propped against Ram's leg to hold himself up while he laughed. Riley had to jump out of the way as Sarge rolled over on his side. Harriet buried her giggling head in Brock's feathers, and even he cracked a smile at the silly scene.

"She seems accident-prone," said Brock. "Sarge, are you certain she can do the kind of work we do?"

"I would not have recommended her if I wasn't sure,"

replied Sarge. "Sometimes accidents lead to unexpected rewards, and Copper has a knack for coming out of her mishaps just fine. Often, what looks like clumsiness is just evidence that someone is trying to do something new. If it means we're attempting to improve, I'm all for more clumsiness in the world."

"I don't see how getting random body parts stuck in things means she's attempting to improve," said Brock.

"Honey, she wouldn't have gotten anything stuck if she hadn't taken a chance to come out here," said Harriet. "Right now, she could be comfortable at home with her humans, like every other house cat. Instead, she chose to come with Riley and Big Strig to see how she could help. I'd say that's a cat who is trying to improve."

"Also, don't forget," added Riley, "she just got you to smile, which is harder than teaching an alligator to fly. That alone proves Copper is capable of amazing feats!"

"Thanks, Riley," said Copper, "but what does Sarge mean by recommended—" She paused as a light flickered across the junkyard causing the dark shadows of wrecked vehicles to dance across the trees. The crows began their clamor again, but the calls sounded different, less like an alarm, and softer, more like a friendly greeting.

What You Crowing About?

Crows sometimes use sentries, crows that are on guard to alert others about something dangerous. Researchers have found that crow communication is more complicated than simple danger alerts, though. Crows can recognize the calls of others in their own family group. They also can make assorted clicks and rattles, besides the familiar cawing sound. In addition to the sounds they make, the number and length of their calls may also be part of crow communication.

Crows have also shown the ability to remember faces, use tools, and even play tricks on each other. Crows are super intelligent! Even the grumpy ones, like Brock.

Learn more at distractfacts.com/cawme.

Copper looked to Brock and Harriet, wondering if she should panic about the light and the cawing. "Should we hide?" she asked.

"We don't need to hide," said Brock. "You're about to meet your ride for tonight."

8

TIME TOW MEET KYLE

Kyle Hammond was on his way to investigate yet another commotion in his junkyard. Only a few minutes had passed since he had returned from an accident call, parked his flatbed tow truck, and found his crazy goat with a leg stuck in the gate. Again. He had freed the goat (while holding an arm across his nose) and let his stinky companion into the junkyard. The gate was there to keep crooks out, but it sure wasn't any good for keeping goats in.

After freeing the goat, Kyle had barely made it to his little farmhouse when a loud bang in the junkyard got his attention. Strange noises in the darkness would frighten most people, but it wasn't in Kyle's nature to panic easily. Growing up, his mom was always reminding him not to create drama, because life will bring you drama enough. Kyle had towed away enough wreckage from plenty of accident scenes to know that was the truth.

Plus, he knew that it wasn't likely that the noise meant a thief was in the junkyard. It was going to be the animals. *Won't be getting much sleep tonight*, Kyle thought as he grabbed a flashlight from his truck.

Sleep had been in short supply since his grandpa had left him the auto repair and salvage business. When he took over the business, Kyle had expected to deal with late-night calls to accident scenes, but that wasn't the problem. The problem was the group of animals that hung out in his junkyard.

As he loped toward the gate, Kyle wondered if his grandpa had ever met those extraordinary animals. It didn't seem likely. It was the sort of thing his grandpa certainly would have told him about. As a child, Kyle spent his afternoons, weekends, and summer days at Grandpa Hammond's side because his parents worked night shifts. During that time, Grandpa Hammond had taught Kyle how to fix just about anything that had an engine in it. They had even fixed a helicopter once for a local tour company whose owner knew his grandpa had worked on choppers in the Army. Grandpa Hammond had taken the time to teach Kyle how to fix a helicopter. Surely, he would have taken the time to tell him about the animals.

Arriving at the gate, Kyle held the flashlight between his teeth while he fumbled with the gate's lock. The chain clanged against metal as he pushed it open, setting off the crows, as usual. Hundreds of them had started to roost in the trees in the months after Grandpa Hammond had died. They made an unbelievable racket at times, but otherwise, they seemed like ordinary crows to Kyle.

However, there was something extraordinary about the pair of crows that hung around the old-fashioned ice cream truck in the junkyard. Those two weren't like any crows Kyle had ever seen, and he wasn't surprised that the noise he heard this evening came from that direction. A lot of bizarre things had been happening around that ice cream truck.

Kyle had many fond memories of that old truck. His grandpa had kept a couple of nylon-strapped lawn chairs inside of it, and on many evenings, he would set them out in the clearing next to the truck and look up at the night sky. It was his grandpa's favorite spot to relax and take a break from manmade creations. Sitting together, Kyle and his grandpa would listen to the sounds of nature in the woods all around them. Grandpa Hammond could identify the sound of every owl, frog, toad, or insect calling in the darkness; he taught Kyle how to recognize them, too.

If he was in a certain mood, Kyle's grandpa would also carry a worn hardback book with him, set a propane lantern on the ice cream truck counter, and read Robert Frost poems aloud beneath the stars. Robert Frost had been Grandma Hammond's favorite. Those nights had been magical to Kyle. The only thing that hadn't been magical about those nights was the smell. His grandpa kept a couple of goats in the junk-yard to help keep the weeds under control, and the male goat reeked like a landfill with horns.

The Original Weed Trimming Machine
Like many grazing animals, goats will eat grass, but what they most crave is the weedy, brushy stuff that people don't want around. Farmers, utility companies, neighbor-hoods, and even junkyard owners use goats to get rid of unwanted vegetation, without the need for chemicals like herbicides. There are even companies that rent out herds of goats for people in need of the bearded brush-clearing bleaters.

You can rent a goat for that yard chore, but a rhyming goat
will cost you more.

Learn more at distractfacts.com/goatgardening.

THAT MALE GOAT had followed Grandpa Hammond everywhere. Sometimes the goat would even lie down next to the
lawn chairs, like he was listening to the poetry. Kyle always
wondered how his grandpa could read with his mouth open
while the putrid fragrance steamed off the goat. After Grandpa
Hammond passed away, the goat became Kyle's shadow. Kyle
actually liked the goat, but he had pondered wearing a gas
mask when it was nearby.

The crows continued their clatter as Kyle arrived at the ice
cream truck. When he shined his flashlight around the clearing
where he had spent so many evenings with his grandpa, Kyle
was not surprised to find his goat and the two peculiar crows
sitting there. As usual, they had a few odd friends hanging out
with them. There was the black tomcat he had often seen
hanging around. Also joining the group was the great horned
owl that always had a green tree frog at its side. Kyle used to
wonder why the owl had not eaten that frog, but after a while,
he realized nothing was ordinary about the animals in his
junkyard.

This time, there was also a second owl with them that Kyle
had never seen before. Its chest was white with streaks of
brown, and Kyle thought it might be a barred owl. It was odd
to see the two types of owls so close together, but that still
wasn't the oddest thing in the clearing. That honor went to an
orange tabby cat wearing a purple walking harness.

The cat looked a lot like the one Kyle thought he had seen earlier, flying across the highway in the grips of an owl. The only difference was the cat he had seen earlier had a plunger stuck on its foot. This cat had a piece of rusty tailpipe stuck on its nose.

"Do you need some help with that, little fella?" He bent down to remove it and Copper backed away.

"What did he say?" she asked.

"We don't know, but he's probably trying to help you," reassured Harriet. "He's a nice human. You can trust him."

Kyle sat back on his haunches as one of the crows cooed. He wondered if it might be communicating with the cat somehow. Copper stepped closer to him and he held out a hand, so she could rub against it. She bumped his hand with her head, and then Kyle stroked the back of her neck. "Let me get that thing off," he said as he eased the busted tailpipe from her face. Copper immediately sat down, licked the side of her paw, and began rubbing it against her nose.

"You obviously belong to somebody, little buddy," said Kyle. He spun his baseball cap backwards so he could read the tag on her collar. "Looks like your name is Copper. There's a phone number, too." He scooped her up and turned to the motley moonlight meeting of animals in his junkyard. "I've never seen y'all with someone's pet before. Is that what you want me to help with this time? Do you want me to help this cat get home?"

Squirming in Kyle's arms, Copper looked to Sarge for help. "Why did he pick me up? What's he saying? How does he know the name my humans gave me?"

"I'm not sure," said Sarge. "Just try to stay calm, little one. We'll get things figured out."

The two crows began making rattling sounds which Kyle

had heard many times before. He assumed they were talking to each other although he didn't have a clue what they were saying.

"Do we have the token?" Brock asked Harriet.

"One of the sentries delivered it earlier today. I've hidden it in one of my stash spots," Harriet replied.

X Marks the Spot. Or Does It?

Like squirrels storing away nuts for winter, crows, ravens, and other birds in the family group called corvids excel at hiding food for munching later. This behavior is called caching. The birds have a remarkable ability to remember where they stashed food. They will even fake like they are making a cache if they think other birds are watching, and then stash the food somewhere else.

Food isn't the only thing that crows cache. They collect pebbles, shells, shiny things, or anything else they find interesting. In some cases, they have left some of those trinkets as gifts for humans who have fed them.

There is no record of famous crow pirates with buried treasure, but arrrr wouldn't put it past these bright birds, mateys.

Learn more at distractfacts.com/crowbeard.

"Do you think he will understand the token?" Brock wondered.

"Well, they picked it up outside of the human place where Benny lives," said Harriet, "and it has the thing that always makes him say 'photo.' I'll go get it."

"Hurry!" urged Sarge. "I don't know what the human is doing, but if he takes her to a shelter, we may never find her again!"

"I'll be back in a jiffy," Harriet replied, already in flight. "My stash spot is just a few flaps away, but no peeking!"

Kyle smiled as he watched one of the crows fly off and silently congratulated himself for so easily discovering what the animals wanted. "This might be the quickest I've been able to figure out what y'all need," said Kyle. "Okay, Copper, I'll take you back to the house. You can hang out there until the morning and then I'll give your owners a call." Kyle turned and started to walk back to his farmhouse.

Copper panicked and wrestled to free herself. "Where is he taking me?" cried Copper. "I don't want to go! I want to stay with all of you!"

"Easy there, fella," Kyle whispered as the cat mewled and struggled in his arms. "I'm not going to hurt you."

"Don't worry, Copper," called Riley. "Harriet will be back in a moment and everything will be fine."

"Just wait for the crow and you won't have to go!" Ram proclaimed.

But Copper was too upset to hear them. She hissed and growled at Kyle as she fought to escape.

"Why don't we make him put her down?" asked Bart. "She's obviously frightened!"

"We don't want to do anything that will make him fearful of us," replied Brock. "He's been a huge help to our squad."

The tree frog calling, goat bleating, and owl hooting got

Kyle's attention, and he turned around just in time to see the barred owl swooping toward his face.

"No! Don't do that!" Brock yelled at Bart.

But it was too late. As Bart flashed by his head, Kyle ducked, losing his hat and his grip on Copper, who immediately sprinted back to the clearing to join the other animals. At the sound of Brock's cry, the sentinel crows took flight with a roar of caws and flapping wings that sounded like a windstorm blowing through the junkyard. Like oil spilled on the night sky, crows streamed from the trees. Bart tried to circle back to join Copper, but the sentinels would not allow him, mobbing him again with some hurling themselves into his wings while others tried to peck at him. The crows continued mobbing Bart until he disappeared deep into the woods, racing for safety among the trees.

Kyle stayed crouched with his hands covering his head until the roar of caws became a smattering of croaks and squawks. "What was that all about?" he said to himself as the chaos in the junkyard settled down.

"What was that all about?" said Harriet, returning to the clearing from her stash spot and dropping something from her beak.

Brock nodded toward Copper, who sat at Sarge's side, nervously swishing her tail back and forth and stirring up little clouds of dust behind her. "Copper was getting upset, so the barred owl did something foolish," Brock explained with his wings upraised. "He charged at the human to make him let her go. I told the owl we didn't want to frighten the human!"

Harriet stretched her neck at Brock and pulled her wings to a point behind her back. "Let me get this straight," she demanded. "Bart tried to help Copper, you thought that was foolish because it would frighten the human, so you commanded hundreds of sentinels to swarm Bart *and* the human?"

Brock dipped his head. "I didn't send the sentinels. They just reacted when I yelled at Bart. They thought I was alarming him as a threat."

"Of course they did, dear. They see us as family leaders. If you yell at something, they'll react and defend us like any natural crow would."

"As soon as I yelled, I realized my mistake, but it was too late by then." Brock looked toward Kyle. "I just didn't want the owl to scare the only human we've ever had help us."

Kyle calmly got to his feet and fetched his hat, then checked the scratches the little tabby cat had left on his forearms. He nodded his head and half smiled as he once again approached the little group of chattering animals. "Evidently, I misunderstood what you needed. You know, this would be a lot easier if you would just speak up." He noticed the second crow had returned during all the pandemonium. There was something laying on the ground near its feet, so Kyle walked over and stooped to pick up the item. "If you won't talk to me, this is the next best thing. I love it when y'all bring me clues I have to figure out! Let's see what you have this time."

Kyle wondered if the crow had buried the item somewhere because it was speckled with dirt. He brushed the dirt away to reveal a glossy brochure. "Hog Island Resort," Kyle read aloud. "I know where this place is. It's across the Ravenel Bridge near Patriots Point. Y'all looking to take a vacation?" He grinned as he looked around at each of the creatures, half expecting them to laugh at his goofy joke. Instead, all he heard was a chirping cricket. And that was because the orange tabby was chasing one around, trying to catch it under its paw.

"Copper, I'm glad you calmed your frazzled nerves, but you might want to pay attention," said Sarge.

"Huh? Oh, sorry!" Copper stopped mid-pounce. "Hard not to get distracted when I see something jumping around like that. I'll try to concentrate." And she did. Copper sat at attention like a little feline soldier for almost a full two seconds . . . until the cricket wriggled out from beneath her paw and she pounced on it again.

Kyle chuckled at the sight of Copper's cricket quest, then knelt and tried to make eye contact with the pair of crows. He held up the brochure. "Is this where the cat needs to go? Are her owners there?" The crows didn't respond; they kept tilting their heads and watching Kyle. So, he looked to the other animals for a response. His goat was nipping at a patch of weeds near the ice cream truck. The black cat was sitting there, blinking. The orange tabby was chasing a cricket again. The tree frog was not moving eyes nor mouth although Kyle always thought it looked like it was smiling. The big owl was staring silently, but then he had never made a sound in all the times Kyle had seen him.

Trying his luck again with the crows, Kyle motioned toward Copper and then pointed at the brochure. "Do I need to take the cat to the place in the photo?"

"There we go!" exclaimed Harriet. "He said 'photo' again. He knows what we need him to do." She patted Brock on the back with one of her wings.

The crow that had brought the brochure made a rattling sound and flapped a wing at Kyle. He thought he might have figured it out. "I'm going to try to pick the cat up again. Please don't have any owls or crows try to eat me," Kyle said as he tiptoed toward the cat, who was now halfway under the pickup trying to reach the cricket.

"Copper!" hollered Riley. "We think he knows what we need. You need to go with him."

Copper shimmied out from beneath the truck. "Where are we going?" she asked.

The tree frog momentarily disappeared from Copper's view as Big Strig stepped over Riley and then clutched him in his talons. Kyle watched as the owl and tree frog lifted off and flew in the direction of his house, the frog chirping loudly from the sky.

"You're going on your first mission for the FLOCC!" Riley cried.

9

OWLS DON'T LIKE COUNTRY MUSIC

K yle picked up the orange tabby cat, holding her away from his body as if he was lifting a little furry chainsaw that might rip into his arms again, and watched as all the other animals scattered. When he turned to leave, he noticed something strange resting on the ground near the ice cream truck. It was the business end of a plunger. "Ha! I bet there is a story behind this thing. I'll have to tell your owners about it if we find them." He cradled Copper in one arm and used the resort brochure to clamp the plunger cup like it was a radioactive toilet tool.

"I'll fix up a spot for you in the kitchen and you can hang out there," yawned Kyle as they walked the path to the farmhouse. "First thing in the morning, we'll call that number on your collar. If that doesn't work, we'll drive out to Hog Island Resort and see if anyone has reported a missing cat." When they reached the junkyard gate, his flatbed tow truck was parked there just as he had left it, but now a great horned owl and a frog were sitting on the hood.

"Climb aboard, Copper!" Riley said in his usual cheerful

voice. She hopped out of Kyle's arms, ran through the gate, and scaled the flatbed to join them.

"Oooookay," said Kyle. "I'm guessing we need to go now instead of later?" The owl, cat, and tree frog just sat and stared. At least the cat was purring.

"Alrighty then." Kyle continued his one-sided conversation with the animals. "Well, I could use a drive to clear my head anyway. You can't ride on the hood though." He opened the door, tossed the brochure and the toxic plunger into the truck, and lifted the cat off the hood. As Kyle slid into the truck with Copper in his arms, the owl whooshed past him with the frog in its talons and settled on the bench seat. Kyle shook his head and laughed. "I'm going to have to get a meter to charge you for trip fares. Next stop, Hog Island Resort!"

The tow truck jerked and shuddered as Kyle fired it up and shifted into gear. He pulled onto the highway with a cat, a tree frog, and a great horned owl as his traveling companions. While Big Strig hopped onto the dashboard, Riley squatted on the headrest to take in the view from the rear window.

"You know, getting a chance to see all this stuff never gets old," said Riley.

Copper stood with her front paws on the passenger side armrest to get a look. Trees zoomed by and her legs felt wobbly. Her head went back and forth like she was watching the world's most extreme ping-pong match. "We seem to be going pretty fast," she said with a tremble in her voice.

"Isn't it awesome?" said Riley. "With this human helping, our squad can get anywhere we need, no matter what type of animal is on the mission. Even a small, but devilishly handsome fellow like me can cover a lot of ground this way."

Copper squinted as they passed the beaming lights of a gas station. "Couldn't Big Strig have flown you?"

"He's taken me to Benny's place a few times." Waving a leg toward the big owl, Riley added, "I don't think Strig has enough muscle to carry you all that distance, though."

Big Strig looked over his shoulder and scowled at Riley. Kyle thought he was finally going to eat the frog.

"Heh, I should say he's plenty strong to do that, but we just don't want to strain the big guy's muscles," clarified Riley. "If we hadn't been able to get our human to help, he would have been up to the task. Nothing too tough for old Strig, right buddy?"

Big Strig snorted and swiveled his head forward as the truck slowed to a stop. A stoplight overhead cast a sinister red glow on his feathers. Cringing at the thought of more flight time with Big Strig, Copper nervously added, "Even though I'm certain Big Strig would have had no trouble, I'm glad you arranged for your human to give us a ride. I'm still a bit confused about what we are doing, though. I think I understand that FLOCC animals are different because they can choose to help other creatures, but how do you help?"

Riley hopped from the headrest to Copper's window in a single leap. He climbed up the glass until his bulging eye was just beyond the tips of her whiskers. "The best way to explain what we do is to start with our name," said Riley. "We are the First League of Caring Creatures."

"Hey, you don't mind if I turn on the radio, do you?" Kyle asked without expecting an answer. Big Strig watched as the human tapped a button and a country song blasted through the speakers. Recognizing the first few notes, Kyle was happy to hear his new favorite song from superstar country artist Johnny Jones Johnson Junior. He began to sing along with a voice that sounded like a wolf choking on one of Copper's squeaky toys.

"I miss that truck, like I'm missing youuuuu! I'd hug my dog, but he left me toooooo!"

Big Strig stepped to the edge of the dashboard, leaned over, and turned the radio off with a single peck. So ended the Kyle Hammond Live in the Truck Cab concert performance.

"As I was saying," Riley continued, "we are the First League of Caring Creatures. Our history stretches back beyond my lifetime and even before Brock and Harriet's time. The league was started by a raven named Linnaeus when he first realized he had the choosing ability."

"What's a raven?" asked Copper.

"They're black birds that look similar to Brock and Harriet, but they're larger. They are super smart too, even the ones who don't have the choosing ability."

"How did he realize he had the choosing ability?" asked Copper.

"It started with the grasshoppers," said Riley. "As the story was told to me, Linnaeus realized at a young age that he was aware of things that other ravens weren't. Like a lot of ravens, he loved to eat grasshoppers and there were plenty to go around. But he couldn't stop thinking about taking more grasshoppers. He started to grab them every chance he got, even if he was already full. He kept wondering why the other ravens didn't try the same thing. They seemed to eat until they were full and hide a few for later, but that was all. Only taking what they needed to survive. But Linnaeus kept stashing away every grasshopper he could, whether he needed it or not.

"Before long, he had eaten or stashed every grasshopper around. He watched the other ravens hunt for grasshoppers and come up empty because he had them all. Because he loved grasshoppers so much, he thought having so many would make him happier than he was before. But he realized he wasn't any happier. He decided to dig up one of his stashed grasshoppers and offer it to one of the ravens hunting nearby. As Linnaeus watched as the raven gobbled up the grasshopper, he was stunned to find that he felt a little happier at that moment. He gave a few more away and found the same thing. He was happier and more peaceful when he helped others."

Riley paused, thinking Copper might be distracted again. They were crossing a bridge and the lights of sailboats moored in the river seemed to have her mesmerized. But even as she kept her eyes glued to the gently rocking lights, Copper replied, "If Linnaeus knew he was different from the others, why did he start the FLOCC? How did he know there were any other creatures with the choosing ability?"

"He didn't know if there were others," Riley answered, "but his own behavior had scared him. It had been too easy for him to make a choice that served only himself and harmed others.

If there were other animals who had the choosing ability, he wanted to find them and tell them what he had learned about choosing to help others. He knew if they had the choosing ability like him, that it would make sense to them once he explained it."

"How did he go about finding them?" asked Copper.

"The same way we find new FLOCC members to this day," said Riley. "Linnaeus started to look for creatures who did something that wasn't for their own survival. If he saw an animal helping another without an obvious reason, Linnaeus supposed they might have the choosing ability and he would try to talk to the animal. New FLOCC members would often notice other animals doing something selfless, and then would recruit those animals to join the organization. The FLOCC has been growing that way ever since."

As Copper nodded her understanding, an astonishing thought popped into her head. "Riley, back there at your headquarters, Sarge said something about *recommending* me. Does he think I have the choosing ability?"

"Yes, he does. He and Callie have been looking for a while, and you're the first house animal he has ever brought to us. He must have seen something special in you."

Copper jerked her head and Riley gripped the glass to keep her eye whiskers from sweeping him off the window. "Wait a minute. Sarge and Callie were working . . . together? She's part of the FLOCC?"

"Yep, she's been part of the squad a lot longer than I have," replied Riley.

"So, she's not really as mean as she acted at the shelter?"

"That's no act. Callie is grumpier than an alligator with a toothache. I think every animal she meets annoys her in some way," said Riley.

Copper wondered what an alligator was, but there was a more confusing question on her mind. "If she doesn't like other animals, why is she working with the FLOCC? I thought the whole purpose was to help other animals. Why would she do that if she doesn't like them?"

"It isn't that she doesn't *like* the animals," Riley answered. "They just don't always act the way she thinks they should, and their behavior annoys her. I don't think you'll find another creature in the FLOCC who loves the cause more than Callie. She would give her left eye to help an animal if an assignment called for it. Heck, she almost did on one of our missions."

"What do you mean she almost did—"

"To give you an example," Riley continued, "she dislikes humans because of her own experience with them. But she's gotten herself locked up in that shelter about as many times as I can count on my hind toes. She was the only cat who stayed behind when Ram busted Sarge out of the shelter, so we could keep track of who adopted you. She's done those things to help the FLOCC find out if Sarge's idea will work. If it works, our whole world is going to change big time and hopefully for the better."

"What's his idea?" wondered Copper.

"It was inspired by Ram and this human," said Riley as he waved a foot at Kyle. "When Ram joined the FLOCC, he told us he thought the human who feeds him might have the choosing ability. We knew humans kept animals as pets, but we figured they just did that for themselves, so we thought Ram was joking about a human having the choosing ability. But Ram said he wasn't joking, that he had seen this human help other animals. Of course, Ram didn't say it that way, he said something like, 'I don't mean to amuse, this human can choose.'"

"That goat does have a way with words," Big Strig abruptly added. Kyle nearly swerved into a lamppost when the usually silent owl suddenly hooted from the dashboard.

"Uh yeah, Strig, he sure does," said Riley. After Copper hopped back to the seat from the floorboard, Riley continued. "Ram was new to the group, and we didn't know how good he was at spotting the choosing ability. None of our leaders had been around humans enough to know, so we decided to set up our headquarters at Ram's place and watch the human. After we saw how well he treated Ram, we tried to figure out ways to communicate with him to find out if he would choose to help other animals. Once we discovered a couple methods that worked, like the 'photo' things, he showed every sign that he was a creature who cared about others. As you can see, he's been a huge help ever since."

The truck fell silent as Copper and Riley both turned to look at Kyle. Noticing them staring at him, Kyle gave a nervous wave. Then the cat turned back to the window as the tree frog resumed chirping.

"When we realized this human could be part of the FLOCC," continued Riley, "we needed to figure out a way to identify any other humans like him. That was when Sarge got the idea for the House Animal Project. When he was a kitten, he had spent some time in one of those places humans call a 'shelter,' and he knew humans came there to get house animals. So, Sarge thought we could try to identify animals in the shelter with the choosing ability. Then, when those animals were taken home by humans, they would be able to tell us more about how their humans communicate and whether they could be potential FLOCC members."

"And I was the first house animal Sarge believed might be a FLOCC candidate?" Copper asked, her eyes wide.

"Yep, but as you might have noticed, Brock wasn't convinced. Every FLOCC candidate has been observed doing something to help another creature. When you were a kitten, Sarge said you tried to be kind to Callie, even after she had been nasty to you. He was confident that you were a good candidate, but Brock felt like we needed to know more. Even Harriet couldn't convince that stubborn old crow. All FLOCC squads have a leadership team, and if everyone on the team isn't in agreement on a decision, we don't go forward with it. Sarge and Callie have continued to search for house animals that have the choosing ability, but you are the only one he has recommended so far."

"If Brock isn't sure about me, then why did you bring me along tonight?"

"He didn't have much choice. We needed an animal who isn't a known FLOCC member to help us find who is taking Benny's chicks. We think it's a creature targeting Benny on purpose."

"Why would a creature target him?"

"I wish I knew," said Riley. "But after another night heron's chick went missing while Strig was on the watch last night, there is a lot of suspicion inside and outside of the FLOCC. We figured if we brought in an animal that had never been seen, it might catch the perpetrator off guard. You were the only animal we could think of that might help and wasn't already known by everyone."

Before Copper could ask why there was suspicion, Kyle veered onto the access ramp for the Ravenel Bridge. Copper sunk her claws into the seat to keep from tumbling onto the floorboard again. Kyle sped onto the bridge, passing a billboard advertising the Johnny Jones Johnson Junior concert in town that night.

The tow truck was an ant marching across the great bridge. Two colossal diamond-shaped towers loomed overhead with massive white cables stretched like harp strings down to the roadway. The harbor below was a silky black tablecloth illuminated by the lights of the USS Yorktown aircraft carrier, blinking channel markers, and a cruise ship docked for the evening. Copper's mouth hung open at the sights outside her window.

"Pretty amazing, isn't it?" said Riley after giving Copper a moment to take it all in. He motioned a foot toward the water. "We've got FLOCC members down there too, by the way."

Copper wanted to say something, but she couldn't think of any words. Then she remembered what Sarge had told her when she was a kitten. *You don't know it yet because you haven't been out of this shelter, but the world is much bigger than the little parts where we make our homes. Everywhere is not the same as your somewhere.* She was beginning to understand the truth in that.

They arrived at the Hog Island Resort and the packed parking lot surprised Kyle. Although the summer tourist season hadn't started yet, business seemed to be booming at the resort. He parked in the closest spot he could find, alongside a walking path at the back of the lot.

"I'm going to run into the office and find out if anybody has reported a missing cat, unless one of you has a better idea," Kyle said to his fellow travelers. The stoic owl surprised him when it leapt off the dashboard and onto the seat with a few hoots and wing flaps.

"Look where we are, Riley," said Big Strig. "We need to get out of sight. If I'm spotted, it could mean the end for Benny."

Seeing the tough owl acting all jumpy puzzled Copper. "What do you mean it could mean the end for Benny?" she asked.

"Strig is right," said Riley. "He and I need to vanish quickly. We'll try to keep an eye on things from a distance if we can. There isn't time to explain but find Benny and he can give you the details."

"But—," Copper started.

"I got a hoot, a frog peep, and a meow, so I'll take it that you all agree with my idea," said Kyle. "I'm sure the desk clerk will think I'm losing my mind, which is the usual response I get when I'm trying to help y'all." Lifting his baseball cap to rub his forehead, he added, "Be right back."

Owl, frog, and cat all watched as Kyle cracked the windows to let in some air, hopped out of the truck, and walked over to the resort office. Other than the soft rattle of the idling diesel engine, the parking lot was eerily silent.

"Okay, gotta go," Big Strig said as he hurried over to the driver's side door. Pecking at the same button Kyle had used, Strig opened the window and a waft of salty air filled the cab. Riley loped over and Big Strig grasped him in his talons.

"Don't leave yet!" Copper exclaimed. "Where do I go to find Benny?"

"You're already there," said Riley, "you just need to—"

Big Strig launched himself out of the window and streaked away from the tow truck. Copper stood on the door and watched her two new friends disappear into the night sky. She was alone in a place she had never been. She had no idea what to do. "I guess I'll try to find Benny," she sighed. She licked her sore paw and cut her eyes at the plunger cup lying on the floorboard. *Hopefully finding Benny will be easier than everything else has been tonight,* she thought. *Wait a minute, I don't even know what a black-crowned night heron looks like!*

10

CAUTION, BARF AHEAD

As he strolled past the brochure dispenser in front of the resort office, Kyle pondered how to ask the front desk clerk if anyone was missing a cat, a cat that he had found on the other side of town. He ran several ideas through his head, but each one seemed likely to result in the clerk thinking he was insane. Best not to mention that owls, crows, and a frog had sent him—guaranteed checkmark next to the insane box. He decided that a little small talk with the clerk would help set the insane-o-meter reading close to zero, and he would have to wing it from there.

Finding an empty front desk, Kyle felt a sense of relief. "Oh well. Guess I'll just head home and see if I can find Copper's owners in the morning," he mumbled to himself as he turned to leave.

"Hello there," called a voice behind him. "Sorry, I was in the back office doing some paperwork. What can I do for you?"

Kyle spun around and saw a pudgy, baby-faced man standing behind the counter. The man's hair looked like it was in a perpetual state of bedhead. His meager mustache looked as if he had been cultivating it for years with only a dusting of lip hair to show for his efforts.

"Uh, hi," replied Kyle. He needed to work in his small talk. "Man, y'all must be slammed. I had to park by the walking path at the back of your lot. I hope that's okay."

"Don't get me started on the parking," the man grumbled. He pounded the stapler into a stack of documents and slid them into a manila folder. "I've petitioned the city to expand our lot, but they say I can't disturb that crazy bird colony near where you parked." He waved a hand toward the parking lot. "We get a slew of one-star reviews saying, 'great resort— terrible parking' and 'our van was plastered with bird poop.' Those blasted birds are costing me business."

"You're the owner of the resort?"

"Yes, I'm sorry. I should have introduced myself. It's been a while since I've worked the night shift at the front desk." He offered a handshake over the counter. "My name is Julius Swine."

"Nice to meet you, Mr. Swine." Kyle stifled a chuckle as he shook the Hog Island Resort owner's hand. "My name is Kyle Hammond. What's got you working the late shift tonight?"

"Four simple words," griped Swine as he popped up four sausagy fingers, one by one, "Johnny. Jones. Johnson. Junior. Somebody gave my night manager tickets to his concert, and she said she'd quit if she couldn't have the night off."

"Wow!" said Kyle. "I can't say that I blame her. I heard he puts on a good show."

"We might have to disagree on that one," Swine groused. "Personally, I think he's been overplayed. Everywhere I go, that 'No Truck, No Lady, No Dog with Me' song is blaring. Drives me nuts!"

"Heh, you definitely wouldn't want to ride with me then," said Kyle. He'd had his fill of small talk with Swine. "Look, I know you're busy, so I don't want to waste any more of your time. I just found an orange tabby cat . . . nearby. I wanted to check to see if it belongs to one of the resort guests. The name Copper is on its collar."

"A cat?" Swine crossed his arms and his face puckered like he'd smelled something awful. "We are a pet-friendly resort, but usually, people bring tiny little dogs with them. You know, the kind they put sweatshirts on and push around in strollers. I haven't seen too many cats."

"Right, I figured it was a long shot, but I wanted to check." Turning to leave, Kyle added, "Thanks for your time."

"Hang on," groaned Swine, rubbing his brow and exhaling an annoyed gust which fluttered the yellow sticky notes framing the computer screen. "The last thing I need is a one-star review about somebody losing their pet here. Half our business probably comes from those tiny-dog people." Swine dragged a metal stool across the floor and settled down in front of the monitor. "If it was reported earlier today, it would be in our lost and found file on the computer. Let me check real quick." He tapped across the keys and waited a few seconds. He tried again. And again. "Just great," Swine moaned. "They've changed the password and didn't tell me. It's got to be on one of these." He began to pluck the sticky notes off the screen like petals on a daisy.

While Kyle was enjoying the pleasant company of Julius Swine, Copper had been pacing on the bench seat in the tow truck. Over and over she would place her front paws on the window, wiggle her rear end to prepare for a jump, and then climb back down to the seat. It wasn't the jump that worried her. It was whatever she would find once she landed. "I came here to help," she told herself. "I'm going to help. I wanted adventure. This is certainly an adventure. Let's do this."

One more time she scaled the door, and one more time she retreated to the seat. She had not reached ninja-level pep-talk skills. Copper had never considered that she might have to go it alone on an adventure. She hung her head and contemplated giving up and waiting for the human to come back. As Copper looked down, she spotted the plunger cup on the floorboard, mocking her defeat. *I've come too far just to end up hiding in here,* she thought. *Sarge believes in me, and I've got to show Brock that Sarge was right. I CAN help Benny and the FLOCC.*

Once more, Copper backed across the seat, but this time, she sprinted toward the door and bounded out of the window. Triumphantly, Copper sailed through the air, only to end her glorious moment with a magnificent crash-landing, right into the spiny fan-shaped leaves of a saw palmetto shrub. "Yeowwww!" she wailed as the plant's thorny spines stabbed her legs. Springing from the bush and landing with jelly-legs on a nearby wooden railing, Copper dug her claws into the wood to keep her balance.

Copper found herself on a walkway which flanked a small pond ringed by trees and dense shrubs. With her ears standing straight, she tuned in to the assortment of new sounds resonating all around her. Tree frogs called, some sounding like Riley, yet others used chirps and peeps that sounded altogether different. Above the din of the tree frogs, southern toads trilled together from all around the pond.

Southern Serenade

When the weather starts to warm in the Southeastern United States, nighttime is the right time to tune in to the sweet sounds of the southern toad (scientific name *Anaxyrus terrestris*). Using a special vocal sac under their throats to make their calls, the males croon and the females swoon when they hear the steady trills from the fellas.

Now, you might be wondering just what a southern toad sounds like. The first thing that comes to mind is a toad saying something like, "I'm fixin' to hop in this water y'all." But southern toads don't sound like that at all. Grab yourself a referee whistle and then blow slow and steady, like you're calling a foul, but you don't want to wake the baby up. That is the sound of a southern toad.

Learn and hear more at distractfacts.com/toadtones.

COPPER TWITCHED an ear toward the thick foliage overhanging the far end of the walkway. Something was moving around in there. Leaves rustled. Branches creaked. She crept along the railing, stopping every few steps to sniff unfamiliar scents in the night air. As she edged further down the railing, the parking lot lights threw Copper's shadow across the foliage. The rustling stopped. When she took another cautious step, Copper saw light reflected from something small and shiny, gleaming within the leaves. Copper never could help herself when it came to small, shiny things. She darted down the railing and poked her face into the leaves to investigate.

Hidden within the leaves, a few bowl-shaped nests made of sticks rested at the intersections of several branches. A small, spiky-haired bird stood on one of the branches at the edge of a nest, inches from where Copper poked her head through. The bird had brownish wings, dappled with white speckles hung in rows like Christmas lights. Its chest was fluffy-white, streaked with brown feathers as if it had been eating a fast-melting chocolate ice cream cone. Copper's gaze shifted from the bird's thick, pointy bill back to the shiny yellow eye that had lured her in. "Hi," she whispered. "I'm looking for someone named Benny. Do you know where I can find him?"

The bird stood motionless, as if it hoped Copper hadn't seen it. Then its pale-yellow feet began to tremble and its whole body started shaking. As the bird's chunky bill flapped open, Copper leaned in, expecting an answer to her question.

But instead of answering, the bird threw up all over her.

And the bird was obviously well fed.

"Ah, grooooosssss!" Copper shouted. Blinded by the barf, she thrashed her head around, retreating from the tree. An empty nest toppled down on her head, spilling feathers all over her that stuck to her fur like puke-plastered plumage. She scrambled back down the railing, but before she could even think about the disgusting possibility of having to lick herself clean, something heavy landed on her back. A sharp object jabbed into the back of her neck as Copper flattened herself against the railing and tried to wriggle free, but she couldn't escape. She was pinned down.

"You picked the wrong nest to mess with tonight, mister," shrieked a high-pitched, squawky-sounding voice. "Hey, everybody! I caught the predator!"

Copper tried to speak but a feather that was stuck on her nose kept getting sucked in each time she opened her mouth. "I'm—PFFFFT—not—PFFFFT—predator!" she sputtered as she heard the flapping of wings and soft thuds of bird feet landing on the railing around her.

"Attack the predator! Attack the predator!" the birds squawked.

Copper tried to struggle to her feet, but the bird on her back dug in with its claws, gripping Copper's walking harness like a saddle. The other birds were screeching like mad and poking at her with their bills. With one paw, Copper swatted at them and tried to retreat down the railing, but more bills snapped at her from behind. One of the birds nipped her poofy tail. "Owwww!" Copper howled, and as she did, she sucked the feather on her nose right down her throat. That was the final straw. With the bird still holding its grip, Copper leapt off the railing to the ground. "I'm not the predator!" she wheezed. "I'm here to help Benny! The FLOCC sent me!!"

"Everyone stop!" shouted the bird on her back. One by one the other birds ceased their shrieking, as the leader walked all the way down her back, stepping forcefully on her head as it hopped off to face her. He was as tall as Big Strig, although not as burly, and his thick, powerful bill was much longer than Big

Strig's. The bird had a scar carved deeply into his bill, giving him the look of a battle tested warrior. But his stubby, skinny legs looked comical, as if they were too small to hold him up. The bird's head sat squarely on his stocky body, making it look as if he had no neck. "Did you say the FLOCC sent you?" croaked the bird.

"Yes," replied a relieved Copper. "I was sent here to help someone named Benny. Do you know him?"

The bird nodded toward the others who, by this time, were standing behind Copper. Each member of the small band flew off with a departing, "Kwak!"

"I know Benny quite well," the leader replied. He watched the others fly out of sight. "It just so happens that he is me. Er, I mean I am me. I mean—"

"Are you Benny?" interrupted Copper.

Benny sighed. "Yes, that's what I mean. I'm a little bit frazzled. What's your name?"

"My name is Copper."

"Copper?" Benny stood on one foot while he used the other to claw at an out-of-place feather on his cottony-white belly. He studied her, his spooky red eyes gleaming in the streetlights.

Not a Chip Off the Old Block

If you see a juvenile black-crowned night heron standing next to an adult, you might not realize they are the same kind of bird. The youngsters can be similar in size to the adults, but they have brownish feathers speckled with white spots. The adults have gray wings, a whitish belly, and the signature black feathers atop their heads which give them their name.

Even the eye colors are different. Juveniles typically have yellow eyes and the grown-ups have spooky-looking red eyes.

Juvenile night herons are not afraid to make silly faces because, when their parents tell them their faces will stick like that, they know it can't be true.

Learn more at distractfacts.com/sillyherons.

"I've never heard of anyone in the FLOCC named Copper," Benny continued. "I know a couple of creatures who look like you, but they don't have that"—he pointed a wing at her walking harness—"What is that you are wearing?"

"This is something my humans put on me when they take me outside."

"You have humans that take you outside?" asked Benny. "Where are you when you aren't outside?"

Copper scrunched her nose as she tried to think of a way to explain.

"Never mind," said Benny. "Are you a new member of the FLOCC?"

Sitting on her hind legs and curling her tail around her front paws, Copper realized that she had bits of loose fur hanging off her tail. Although she really, really wanted to lick it, she tried not to get distracted. "I'm not a member of the FLOCC, but Riley brought me here to help you . . . somehow."

"Riley is here?" asked Benny. "Did he bring you for protection this time instead of Big Strig?"

"Huh?" said Copper. "Uh, no—well, yes—I mean—yes, Riley should be here somewhere, but he didn't bring me for protection. Big Strig is with him."

"Oh, no," groaned Benny. "That's not good. Riley should know better than to bring him here after last night."

"Why would having Big Strig here be a bad thing?" asked Copper.

"Because most of the birds here think Big Strig has been killing our chicks," Benny replied.

11

SQUAWK, CACKLE, SQUACKLE

"What?" Copper cried. "Why would they think Big Strig is killing the chicks?"

Benny cocked his head and searched the trees above them. "If Riley brought you here, I think you should already know the answer to that."

"Sooooo, it's been kind of a crazy night and Riley hasn't fully explained what's going on or what I'm supposed to do," Copper replied. "He told me you could give me some details."

"Really? That's odd," said Benny. He opened and shut his beak as if he were going to say something but had changed his mind. "How much do you know about black-crowned night herons?"

Copper pointed a paw at Benny. "I know you're one, and . . . that's about it."

"Okay, I guess I need to fill you in," said Benny. "Black-crowned night herons get together at this place every year because we want to have somewhere safe from predators to build nests and raise our little ones. We call the safe location where we raise kids a rookery. That nest you nosed into is the first nest Betty and I built together, many seasons ago. We've spruced it up each year."

"Who is Betty?" asked Copper.

Benny raised his head high, revealing that he did indeed have a neck. "Betty's my better half," he replied in a higher and squawkier tone than normal. "She and I have raised forty or fifty little ones here over the years. Honestly, I've lost count at this point."

"Ummm, did you say forty or fifty?" asked Copper.

"Yep!" Benny puffed out his chest. "And we hatched five new family members this year—Bonnie, Brady, Brody, Bailey, and Steve."

Copper gave her trademark head-tilt. "Steve?"

"After you've had so many kids, you run out of ideas for names that start with a B," Benny explained. "I can't tell you how many times we've used the name Benny Jr. So this year, we decided to change it up a little, and we went with the name Steve for our youngest. He's named after one of Bettie's uncles. That's Steve you just met."

"Gotcha," said Copper. Then as she continued to think about her meeting with Steve, she had to ask, "Is that how black-crowned night heron chicks usually greet others? It seemed kind of like he threw up on me."

Benny snickered. "Our nestlings do that sometimes. Hopefully it causes a predator to lose its appetite for a black-crowned night heron chick."

Wouldn't a Fist Bump Be Better?

When they are startled, young black-crowned night herons greet intruders by regurgitating food as a defense mechanism. It is an unappetizing way to drive off the predator, or if the youngster's last meal was something tasty, the predator may decide to opt for the instant meal instead of killing the chick.

Thanks to this barfing behavior, researchers can easily get food samples when they're studying the diet of young night herons. The rest of us should simply keep our distance from their nests and ask politely what they had for breakfast.

Learn more at distractfacts.com/grossgreeting.

COPPER LOOKED over her barf-covered fur with clumps of nestling feathers stuck everywhere. She smelled like a combination of wet cat and rotten fish. She grimaced as she took in a breath that was a little too deep for her present state of stink. "I can see how that might work," she said.

"Yeah, but that hasn't been enough to stop the creature who has been taking our chicks." Benny exhaled a long sigh. "Bonnie, Brady, Brody, and Bailey are gone. Steve is all we have left."

"I'm sorry for your loss," said Copper.

"Thank you, Copper, but I haven't given up hope yet." Looking down his long bill at the orange tabby, Benny continued, "I'm not so sure we've lost them for good. At first, we assumed a normal predator was at work, but there is something unnatural about this."

"Something unnatural?" Copper asked. "What do you mean?'"

"For one thing, up until last night, the only chicks taken were my own," explained Benny. "That's somewhat strange with so many other nests here in our colony. Also, there's no evidence that any of the chicks have been eaten, or even any signs of a struggle. It's like they . . . vanished."

"How do you know it isn't just a sneaky predator?" asked Copper.

"It is definitely something sneaky. We've been keeping a watch, but whatever it is seems to be very skilled at hunting undetected. That's why I initially sent word to the FLOCC leaders and asked for Big Strig to come to our rookery. I thought he might be able to catch the predator in the act. If any creature could catch another expert hunter, it would be Big Strig."

Copper nodded. From what she had seen of the brawny, frightening owl, he was the best bird for the job.

"Unfortunately," Benny continued, "last night, while Big Strig was on guard, the predator got one of the other night heron's chicks. It was the first chick taken that wasn't one of mine."

"But why do they think Big Strig is the one who took the chick if he wasn't around the other nights?" asked Copper.

Benny closed his eyes and took a deep breath. "Because one of the night herons, Nick, was feeding in the marsh and he said he saw an owl carrying something away from the rookery. He wasn't sure what the owl was carrying but when he returned, he discovered one of his chicks had gone missing. After he told the other night herons what he had seen, a bunch of them immediately suspected Big Strig. They got together and ran him off."

"That doesn't seem right for them to blame Big Strig," said Copper. "That could have been some other owl that Nick saw. Heck, I've already met two of them, and this is the very first time I've been out at night."

"That's the problem," replied Benny. "As far back as I can remember, we've never lost an adult or a chick to a predator. No one has ever seen an owl around here; that's one of the reasons it has been such a wonderful and safe place for us. Big Strig is the first owl ever seen around here, and the next thing we know, someone sees an owl carrying off one of our chicks. It's only natural that they would suspect him."

"That's terrible!" exclaimed Copper. "*You* don't think Big Strig is the one responsible, do you?"

Benny fanned out his silvery wings in frustration. "I don't know what to think right now," he said. "I don't know why only my chicks were being taken until last night. It's like some creature was targeting Betty and me on purpose. And since I'm the one who brought in Big Strig, the colony now thinks I'm dangerous. They want to abandon this place and kick me out of the colony."

Home Sweet Home

Black-crowned night herons typically nest together, for safety, in groups called colonies. They will abandon nests and sometimes entire colonies if they sense a threat to themselves or their young ones. When an entire colony is deserted, it is called colony abandonment.

Colonies may contain only black-crowned night herons, or sometimes, they share the colony with other birds like egrets or ibises. Some colony sites have lasted fifty years or more!

No studies have been conducted to determine if night herons leave their colony Christmas lights up all year long.

Learn more at distractfacts.com/noplacelikehome.

"EVEN BETTY'S instinct is to leave me," Benny continued in a soft voice, as if he didn't want to hear the words coming out.

"But you said that Betty has been with you for a long time!" Copper exclaimed. "Surely she knows you aren't dangerous!"

"Betty doesn't have the choosing ability," said Benny. "As far as I know, none of the other night herons in our colony have it. Everything they do is based on what gives each of them the best chance of survival. They don't have the capability to recognize there is a purpose in caring for and helping other creatures. If they had the choosing ability, they would understand why Big Strig is helping me, but they're normal wild creatures concerned only with survival. I don't blame them for feeling unsafe when they see me working with a great horned owl; they sense a threat to their survival. The rejection still hurts, though."

Pausing, Benny watched as a handful of colony members flew overhead, in the opposite direction from the nearby river. "There go the scouts," he said. "They're looking for a new location for the colony, and I'm afraid it won't take them too long to find a place with the right qualities. This may be the last night here and my last opportunity to convince the colony that I'm not a threat and that it's safe for everyone to stay. I'd hoped I had the answer when I caught you going into my nest."

"How would that have been the answer?" asked Copper.

"If I can catch the predator, then I can find out what happened to our chicks and maybe show everyone that the rookery can be safe again. At the very least, I could show them I'm not a threat."

Copper watched as a moth flitted by and she thought about pouncing on the moth before bringing her attention back to Benny's problem. "Hey! Maybe I could pretend to be the predator, and you could run me off while some of the others are watching. That would show them you aren't a threat and they would keep you in the colony!"

Benny shook his head. "Thanks for the offer, but that's not going to work."

"Why not?" she asked. "You don't think I could convince them? Beneath my cute exterior lies the heart of a fierce beast." She swiped a paw in Benny's general direction.

Benny squawked and cackled at the same time, something

like a squackle. "I'm sure you could convince them, but I'm going to have to take your word for it on the cute exterior thing. You are looking a bit . . . rough at the moment."

Copper had been so caught up in Benny's story that the sad state of her disgusting, feathery, night-heron-chick-dinner-encrusted fur had slipped her mind. She really, really, needed to start licking, but she really, really didn't want to do it. "That makes it even more believable," she said. "They'll think I'm some sort of funky-looking, never-before-seen predator. You'll run me off and everything should be good again for you. Right?"

"I'd love it to be that easy and I appreciate you offering to help," Benny replied. "But the other night herons who helped me catch you would know you aren't the predator. If I'm going to get this fixed, I think I need to find the true answer. I need to find out who is doing this and what happened to our chicks."

"I see your point," agreed Copper. Glancing up at the trees hanging over the rookery, she wondered if the predator was watching them. A steady breeze picked up, and the moonlight flickered across the swaying treetops. She looked for signs of movement, reflections of eyes, anything that might be a clue that Benny could use, but every leaf and branch danced to the tune of the wind. She had no idea what to look for. "I want to help you, Benny, but I'm not sure how to help or even how any of this outside stuff works. Before tonight, I didn't know anything about crows, owls, rookeries, black-crowned night herons, predators, or . . . anything that wasn't in my house. But I want to help make this better."

The black feathers atop Benny's head stood up like an antenna. "When you look, you see," he said to himself in a loud whisper.

His words sounded familiar to Copper. "What did you say?" she asked.

"Sorry, you reminded me of the FLOCC motto," said Benny. "When you look, you see. It means if we stop and look, we see how all creatures are connected, we see that we should care about each other, and we see ways to do that. Our motto reminds those of us with the choosing ability to look beyond ourselves."

"I like the sound of that. Tell me something I can do to help," said Copper.

"I'm afraid I'm running short on ideas," Benny said with a discouraged squawk. "But I can use all the help I can get. I see why Riley brought you."

"I'm glad somebody sees it. I still don't know why I'm here. For that matter, I don't even know that I have the choosing ability. One of the FLOCC leaders, the crow named Brock, didn't seem to think I should be here."

"That's typical for Brock," said Benny. "He likes to be confident in the character of the creatures he meets. When Riley introduced me as a potential FLOCC member last year, Brock treated me the same way. It takes time for him to give trust."

"How did you meet Riley?" asked Copper.

For the first time in her life, and there had been many firsts in her life already that night, Copper heard a black-crowned night heron laugh. "Ha! Like many of the creatures who know Riley, I was moments away from eating him," Benny explained. "His head hung out the side of my bill, and I was one gulp from swallowing him when he asked me if I wanted to hear a joke."

Copper nodded her head. "I've heard about his famous jokes. What was the one he told you?"

Benny chuckled before he started the joke. "What do you

get when you cross a black-crowned night heron with a yellow-crowned night heron?"

Copper had never heard of a yellow-crowned night heron, but she wasn't going to ask for an explanation and ruin the joke. "I don't know. What?"

"A bumble-bird!" Benny howled for a good ten seconds and then wiped a wing across his brow.

"Whoo! That was a good one," he said after catching his breath. "We had a great laugh, and it made me decide to skip having that special frog for dinner. After I got to know Riley, I realized Big Strig had probably been somewhere close by the whole time, ready to save him if things didn't go well."

"I saw a similar situation earlier tonight when I met Riley," said Copper. "I would think there are better ways to meet new creatures besides nearly being eaten by them, but it seems to be working for him."

"It sure does," Benny replied. "And the more you spend time around the FLOCC members, you'll see there is a reason behind everything they do. Long before my not-so-accidental meeting with Riley, they had been watching me. They had seen something that made them think I was a candidate for the FLOCC."

"Do you know what they saw in you?" asked Copper.

Benny hung his head. "Yes, that was a terrible day I will never forget. Betty and I have a special spot where we like to forage together, a stream that we found a short distance from here in some woods across the river. That day, I saw an owl being attacked and I tried to help her. I had seen the owl with her little one earlier, and I thought of my own young ones. I couldn't do much to help her, but Riley and Big Strig were there and they saw me try to help. That caught their attention.

"Later, when Riley told me they believed I had the choosing

ability, he explained how the FLOCC encourages animals with the choosing ability to care about others. Everything made sense. I had always known that the way I felt about Betty was more than simply having someone to build a nest with. Seeing her happy made me happy. Because I already knew what it was like to care for another creature, Riley didn't have to convince me to join. I was ready to be part of the squad as soon as I heard about it."

"Wow!" said Copper. "You must care a whole lot for Betty."

"I could spend all night telling you how wonderful she is, but here she comes now. You can see for yourself!"

Benny pointed a wing above Copper, and she turned just in time to see a large, black shadow descending from the sky. Copper ducked as a bird that looked like Benny's identical twin swooped down and landed next to him. Although Betty might have been a little smaller, everything else about the two stocky birds looked the same. They both had the black feathers on their heads that made it look like they were wearing bike helmets, silvery wings held at their sides, short yellow legs, glowing red eyes, and that same no-neck appearance with their heads hunched down.

"Benny!" exclaimed Betty. "What has gotten into you lately? You're supposed to be watching Steve, not bringing him out in the open to make it easier for that predator to get him!!"

"What are you talking about, Betty?" replied Benny. "Steve is safe and sound in the nest!"

"Then whose chick do you have out here?" She raised the feathers on her head and stepped closer to Copper for a better look. "Hold on, that's not a chick. That's a—what is that?"

"Betty, this is uh . . . Copper." Benny struggled to come up with a way to introduce her. He couldn't say she was with the FLOCC because the whole Big Strig incident had given the

FLOCC a bad reputation as far as Betty was concerned. Besides, Copper wasn't even an official member of the squad.

"Hold that thought," Betty interrupted, much to Benny's relief. "I just swallowed dinner for Steve and I need to feed him now. I'll be right back." She hustled into the tree where their nest was hidden, and a hungry Steve awaited.

Copper shuddered as she heard Betty heaving up Steve's dinner. "It's weird that she thought I was one of the chicks," Copper said to get her mind off the nearby food preparation.

"I guess, from the air, with you sitting down, those feathers stuck all over your back make you look like . . ." Benny's voice trailed off as he circled around behind Copper. "Copper, I think Betty just gave me an idea for how you can help!"

"Great! What do you need me to do?"

"How do you feel about getting a little wet?"

"Well, actually I had a bath once when I was a kitten and I strongly dislike—" Copper stopped to think about what she was saying. "Never mind. Tell me how I can help."

"Follow me," said Benny, "but walk *slowly*. We're going to try a little technique I use to catch fish from time to time. Only in this case, we'll be trying to catch the creature who has been taking my chicks, and you'll be the bait."

Get That Bird a Bass Boat

Think it sounds fishy that a black-crowned night heron might know how to use bait? It's no fish tale! Black-crowned night herons have been observed placing bits of bread and even dragonflies on the surface of the water, and then snatching the fish who swim up to take the bait. Other types of herons have also been observed using the same baiting technique. It's an amazing example of birds using tools to catch prey!

It isn't common to see this in the wild, so if you see a black-crowned night heron relaxing with its feet on a cooler and a fishing pole in the water, make sure you get a picture. You don't want to have to tell your friends about the one that got away.

Learn more at distractfacts.com/hookedonherons.

12

FISHING WITH FELINES

A s he pulled each yellow sticky note from the computer monitor, Julius Swine slowly constructed a miniature yellow tower. None of the notes contained the magic word he needed to access the office computer, and his agitation was growing by the minute. Kyle thought the keyboard might snap in two as Swine's heavy fingers clacked out all the super extra-strength passwords he could think of.

"HogIsland1 . . . nope . . . HogIsland2 . . . nope . . . HogIsland3 . . . arrgh!" Swine walloped the keyboard with his fist, somehow activating the computer's voice-controlled assistant.

"Hello, how may I help you?" the friendly, disembodied voice offered.

"You can tell me what the password is," muttered Swine.

"You can change your password after you log in," the friendly, yet unhelpful voice replied.

"If I could log in, I wouldn't have to change the password, now would I?" Swine argued.

"I'm sorry, I don't understand your command," replied the ghostly voice inside the computer. "Here are a few commands you can say from the lock screen. Say 'What is the weather tomorrow?' 'What time is it?' or 'Play music.'"

Swine groaned and ran his hands through his hair. Kyle wasn't sure if the man was going to scream or cry, but he thought one or the other was imminent. "Hey, you've got a lot going on," said Kyle. "Don't worry about checking on this right now. I'll just—"

Right then, the desk phone rang. Swine held up a meaty hand to Kyle as he answered. "Hog Island Resort, how may I help you? Oh, I'm sorry about that ma'am. Which unit are you in? Okay, we'll have someone down there right away." He hung up the phone, scraping his metal stool across the floor as he shoved away from the desk.

"So, on top of everything else, I've got a guest with a clogged toilet," Swine whined. "And wouldn't you know, I have no maintenance lady today because of Johnny Jones Johnson Junior."

"Playing Johnny Jones Johnson Junior," announced the computer's voice assistant.

"What? No, I don't want that. Don't Play! Don't Play!" Swine hollered. The computer remained silent for a few seconds, and then the familiar first chords of "No Truck, No Lady, No Dog with Me" blared through its speakers.

Kyle might have been delirious from lack of sleep, but when he heard the music start, he couldn't help himself. He laughed and started to play a little country air guitar. "I've got the business end of a plunger out in my truck if you need it," he shouted above the up-tempo beat of his favorite song. "But I've got no plunger stick, no lady, no dog with meeee!"

Swine's face was blank. It was difficult to tell if the song had finally taken his will to live or if he was trying to sort out why Kyle had the top of a plunger in his truck. "If you happen to know how to make that music stop, I'd appreciate it," he said with a vacant look in his eyes. "I'll be right back." Without a backward glance, Swine hurried out through the rear door, leaving Kyle alone in the lobby.

After jamming to the chorus one more time, Kyle leaned over the counter and turned the speakers down. Yawning as he plopped onto a cushiony faux-leather loveseat, Kyle realized that Swine was having such a terrible night that he probably didn't even realize he'd left the office empty and unlocked. As Kyle rested his head on the back of the chair and closed his eyes, he decided to wait a few minutes for Swine before being on his way. In a matter of seconds, Kyle was snoring softly.

While Kyle ventured into dreamland, Copper followed Benny deep into black-crowned night heron turf. He led her across the railed walkway and down the sidewalk that skirted the pond. Every few steps, Benny stopped and muttered instructions for Copper. "Stay as low to the ground as you can when you walk," he whispered. "Keep to the shadows as much as possible."

They left the sidewalk and eased through the thick shrubs at the edge of the pond. Clouds rode in with the breeze and the moon was veiled, like a flashlight under the sheets. There were no streetlights once they left the sidewalk, so it was easy for Copper to stay in the shadows. She wasn't sure that was a good thing, though. "Hey Benny," Copper whispered on one of their stops. "We aren't anywhere near your nest. How will we catch the creature taking your chicks?"

"Our chicks weren't taken from the nest," Benny replied. He kept his eyes focused on the path ahead. "They disappeared while they were foraging around the pond. When chicks first leave the nest, they still can't fly for a couple of weeks, so they walk around the edges of the rookery. If we walk and stop every so often, I'm hoping you'll look like a chick learning to hunt. Do your best to keep quiet and act like a chick!"

Copper wanted to follow Benny's advice, but it was hard to act like something she knew nothing about. All she knew was to do as Benny told her. Stay low, keep in the shadows, shuffle a few steps, and stop. Shuffle—Shuffle—Stop. Shuffle—Shuffle —Stop. They finally emerged on the other side of the underbrush along the pond bank. As Copper stepped into the mud, it squished between her toes. She flopped down and licked at her paw as if she had stepped on hot coals. "What did I just step on?" she cried.

"Shhhh!" Benny hissed. "What are you doing? You can't sit there licking your feet. Night herons don't do that!"

Realizing her mistake, Copper sprang to her feet and thrust her paw back into the muck. *Be a black-crowned night heron chick, be a black-crowned night heron chick,* she told herself as she stepped through the squishiness.

Copper had never been in a place with so little light. Thick clouds hid the moon and the streetlights' glow only trickled through the trees. She tried to see with her ears the things she couldn't detect with her eyes. Frogs and toads sang all around her. Something sloshed through the water. Hopefully, something friendly.

As she and Benny continued to meander along the edge of the pond, the frogs closest to them halted their songs until the pair had walked past. Each eerie pocket of silence made Copper more anxious. If the predator was out there, she had no way to tell where or what it was. She stopped to listen for any trace of movement. Then she closed her eyes to focus on the unusual sounds floating in the air, hoping that she might detect something suspicious. When she opened her eyes, Copper had lost sight of Benny. She hurried to catch up with him.

"Eeeep!" something nearby cried and splashed into the water ahead of her as Copper dashed toward Benny.

"What was that? Was that the predator?" she whispered loudly as she bumped into Benny in the murk. The blackness made it difficult for her to even see her own tail, but she knew it had to be five times bigger than normal.

"That's a bronze frog," Benny answered calmly. "They squeak and jump when they get spooked."

The Squeaky Frog Scares the Predator

If you've ever been walking along a stream or pond, and you were startled by a high-pitched squeak followed by a splash, it was probably a bullfrog or a bronze frog. The bronze frog is also known as the green frog, depending on where it lives. The bronze ones tend to be bronze or brownish in color, and the green ones are . . . green.

Researchers aren't certain why these frogs do the squeak and splash. Some think the squeak is a way to startle a predator; while others think it's a warning to alert other frogs in the area.

If you haven't walked along a stream or pond, get your grown-ups to take you to a park and try it out. You can enjoy the laughs as you watch the squeaking frogs surprise the adults. You may want to tell them to take a backup pair of underwear, just in case.

Learn more at distractfacts.com/squeakandsplash.

"OH! I suppose if it had a tail, it could poof it instead of squeaking and jumping like that," said Copper.

"If it had a tail, then it would probably be a salamander," Benny replied. "Remember, try to keep quiet. The bait won't work if it looks like bait."

They continued their slow march in silence as drops of water began to tap on the leaves overhanging their heads. "It's only rain," Benny whispered. "We're probably about to get a lot wetter, but the rain will make it harder to see. That should help us."

More wetness. Copper wasn't thrilled about that.

The rain began to fall heavier, buckling the canopy of leaves with each drop. Water stung Copper's eyes and ran down into her nose as it funneled off the leaves. She began to doubt Benny's plan. What if the predator was clever enough to see through her makeshift disguise? What if the rain washed the disguise off? Worse yet, what if the predator truly was Big Strig? He wouldn't make a move now that they suspected him. If Benny's plan didn't draw out the predator, did that make it more likely that Big Strig was guilty?

Copper froze as something rustled in the bushes behind her.

All the frogs around her stopped singing. The hairs on her back raised up and her ears stood tall in the sudden silence. Then, more rustling came from the shrubbery. Copper spun around, arched her back, and got into pouncing position even though she had no idea what she was about to pounce on. Looking over her shoulder for Benny, Copper saw nothing but misty gloom and jumbles of leaves waving at her with each raindrop. She jerked her head back to the bushes, just in time to see a shiny, yellow eye pop out from the foliage.

"SCREEEEEEEE!" the creature shrieked at the sight of Copper.

A glossy, red eye emerged from the thicket behind the creature. "KWAK!" the animal called to its screaming young one.

As Copper began shaking her bottom and preparing to pounce, she realized she had heard that sound earlier. Benny scurried up, causing Copper to flinch as he appeared at her side. "It's okay, Copper," Benny huffed. "That's Nick out foraging with one of his chicks."

Nick was a mirror image of Benny, and his chick was a less spiky-haired version of Steve, brown with streaks of white on its wings and looking nothing like the adult night herons.

"Good evening, Nick," Benny offered. Nick said nothing. He raised the feathers on his head and gave a raspy croak toward his chick. They turned their backs and strolled along the bank in the direction of Benny's nest.

"Not too friendly, are they?" said Copper.

"That's typical behavior," Benny replied. "Nick hardly ever says anything. His chick yelled at you because it assumed you were another chick. They're pretty competitive at that age. You hear hollering like that all around the colony this time of year."

"I guess I must look convincing in my feathers. Even another chick was fooled."

"Yeah, but it doesn't seem like we're fooling our predator, if it's even here tonight." Benny sighed as he looked to the sky. "This rain is pretty steady, and I know you're getting soaked. We should probably head back."

Copper didn't reply; she was watching Nick and his nestling walk along the edge of the water until they disappeared into the darkness. As Copper stood there, she was quite a sight. Her paws were caked with slimy mud. She was drenched to the bone in a disgusting soup of rainwater and partially digested nestling snacks. Around her walking harness, her matted fur was starting to itch, and she had feathers stuck in places where feathers shouldn't be. Well, as a cat, there really shouldn't have been feathers stuck anywhere. "No," she said finally.

"You don't want to go back?"

Copper faced her new black-crowned night heron friend. "I want to go back as much as I'd like a nice warm sunbeam and a bowl piled high with wet food right now. I'm hungry and I'd like something soft to lay on. I'm not sure how I'm going to clean myself, but I know it's going to take a lot of licking. So, yes, Benny, from my claws to the tips of my ears, I want to go back."

Lightning streaked across the sky and Copper thought she

saw something sparkle in the trees above them. "But you could lose everything you love tonight," she continued, "and I'm not going to quit, simply so I can get comfortable. Not when I can truly help. We fooled Betty and we fooled Nick's chick, so I think we still have a chance to fool the predator. Let's do this."

Benny rattled his bill and shook the water from his wings. "Thanks, Copper. Even if things don't work out, I know I've gained a friend."

"Make sure you tell Riley it's possible to form a friendship without having someone try to make a meal out of you first," said Copper. "It seems like the frog thinks that's the only way to do it."

Benny and Copper laughed quietly together in the mud and the rain, until a faraway rumble of thunder rolled. Copper flattened her ears and instinctively looked for her spot under the table where she hid when thunderstorms shook the walls at home. There was no place to hide outside.

"We should get moving," said Benny. "If this storm gets worse, no creature is going to be doing any hunting and we'll run out of time before sunrise."

The pair resumed their slow plodding until they reached the end of the pond. The steep bank forced Copper to walk in the shallow water to keep her balance. Rain pelted them mercilessly. A concrete pipe covered with tall weeds jutted out from the side of the embankment and water flowed from its shadowy mouth. Copper hesitated before stepping near it. They had assumed the predator was some kind of bird, but what if it was something on the ground? What if it was hiding in that pipe? That would explain why there was no sign of the chicks or of a struggle. It, whatever it was, could have taken them right into that pipe and disappeared. She wanted to ask

Benny, but she didn't want to make any sounds that might tip the predator.

Benny showed no fear as he waded by the pipe. Copper was unsure as to whether she could keep her footing in the rolling water, so she decided to cross over the top of the pipe, through the tall weeds. Instantly, she regretted her choice; because the weeds were so high, she couldn't see a thing as she walked. Sitting up, Copper tried to get a better look, but as she did, she felt the stinging pain of something sharp digging into her back.

Before she could turn to look at her attacker, Copper was airborne. The creature grunted and huffed to keep her aloft. It had expected the weight of a black-crowned night heron chick, not a cat.

Copper's paws dragged the water as the creature struggled to get altitude. She twisted her head around to meet the face of her kidnapper. A flash of lightning lit up the pond and Copper gawked at her captor's inky black eyes and hooked yellow bill.

"Bart?"

She was unable to get another word out. The barred owl released its grip, and Copper plunged into the murky pond.

13

GREAT HORNED HEADACHE

Water gushed into Copper's nose and ears like the bursting of a dam. Flailing her legs in a frenzy, she popped her head above the surface. As the water drained from her ears, she heard Benny's voice.

"Riley, don't let it escape! Keep it in the rookery!" Benny cried to the frog soaring overhead and clutched in Big Strig's talons. "We need to catch it and find out what it has done with the others!"

"Help!" Copper gasped. "I'm in the water!" Creatures flew overhead but she couldn't make them out. Each thrash of her legs splashed more water into her face.

"Help is on the way, Copper! Keep your head where we can see you!" Riley shouted from somewhere in the sky.

"Pretty much—no other—choice!" she shouted back between paddles.

Big Strig and Riley swept by. KWAKs, RULPs, and all manner of alarm calls enveloped the rookery as the few night herons who weren't out foraging hunkered down to protect their nests. At one end of the pond, Benny was engaged in aerial combat, trying to keep a barred owl contained within the rookery's tree-lined borders.

"Looks like Benny needs help, Strig," said Riley, "but you're the only one who can rescue Copper. I'll occupy the owl until you get back. Let's try the old Frog Eye Special attack."

Big Strig bolted toward the bird-on-bird battle, releasing the flying frog projectile into the fracas. Riley ploughed into the back of the barred owl while Big Strig banked hard and circled back for Copper.

Riley scampered up the attacking owl's back between wing-beats and climbed onto its head. Then, he covered one of the owl's shiny, black eyes with his shiny, white belly.

"Ahhh! What's on my eye?" the owl screamed. It swatted at its face with one wing and at Benny with the other, like a human thrashing his arms after walking into a spider web.

"Nice one, Riley!" cried Benny as he fended off the owl's furious swats. "For once, someone is getting a look at your stomach instead of you getting a look at theirs!"

"You know I'm all for the jokes," said Riley, "but I don't have a very good grip here." He squeezed his eyes shut as he strained to hold on. "We're going to need something other than my powerful frog muscles to get this bird on the ground. Hurry back, Strig!"

Big Strig hovered over the pond, using his radar-like hearing to locate Copper. He pinpointed the spot where she thrashed in the water, but he could only see her pointy ears.

"Push up from the water!" Big Strig boomed. "I need something I can grab onto!"

"I am pushing!" she panted. She had used her muscles more in this one night than she would in a whole week at home. Her legs burned with fatigue. Her head dipped beneath the surface and water shot straight up her nose. The shock gave her the energy boost to heave herself up one good time. That was all Big Strig needed as the silver leash ring attached to her walking harness flashed into his eye. He dove for it like a heat-seeking missile.

"Gotcha!" he shouted as his talons latched onto the ring. But Big Strig hadn't considered how heavy a drenched cat wearing a saturated walking harness would be. He pumped his wings, and a trail of ripples formed as he skimmed over the water. As they approached the edge of the pond, he thrust his feet forward, releasing his hold on Copper. "That'll have to do! Got to get Riley off that owl!" he cried and whirled around to help Riley and Benny.

Copper landed on her feet but Big Strig had launched her with such momentum she couldn't stop herself. She crashed face-first into the spiny fronds of another saw palmetto bush. "REEYOOOW!" she screamed, tearing a couple of whiskers off as she backed away from the bush. She stepped on a bronze frog who squeaked and leapt into the pond behind her, startling her already shaky nerves. Copper ran as fast as her wet legs would carry her, searching for somewhere safe to hide.

As chaos ensued in the rookery, Julius Swine hurried across the parking lot to his office. He was congratulating himself for conquering his customer's clogged toilet when he noticed a cacophony of cat shrieking, owl growling, wing flapping, and night heron KWAKing coming from the rookery. He trotted over to investigate.

Big Strig had almost reached the barred owl who was twisting, twirling, and climbing high above the trees as it tried to strip off its frog eye patch. Benny flapped all around the owl, trying to force it to the ground where the fight would be more in his favor. The owl turned hard, causing Benny's flailing wing to sweep Riley right off the owl's eye.

Standing in the hazy glow of a streetlight, Swine squinted through the rain. The hair stood up on the back of his neck as he listened to the chaos beyond the trees. Something was crashing through the bushes along the banks of the pond, an assortment of birds was brawling in midair, and a frog seemed to be squealing as well. But since the squeal appeared to be coming from the sky, Swine had to assume he was wrong about that one.

Big Strig raced toward his free-falling friend and plucked him from the sky. But the great horned owl's tremendous speed propelled him over the treetops, and before he could make a turn back for the rookery, he slammed into the side of a steel streetlight.

CLANG!

The streetlight above Swine flickered, a dark object thudded to the ground nearby, and he felt something clammy land on his back. Swine screamed like a pig watching a scary movie and dashed for the office at a speed that even a peregrine falcon might envy.

Cheetahs Got Nothing on Me

When the subject of fast animals is brought up, a lot of people think the cheetah is the champion of speed. With an estimated top speed of 60 to 70 miles per hour, the cheetah is probably the fastest animal on turf, but it looks like a tortoise in quicksand compared to a diving peregrine falcon.

While flying, peregrine falcons can reach about the same speed as a running cheetah, but when these birds dive, they can light up the radar gun with speeds up to 200 miles per hour. These agile aviators dine mostly on other birds and bats, which means they must be quick to catch their chow. Peregrine falcons hover high above their targets before plunging with their wings at their sides and snatching the prey.

Depending on the season, you have a chance to see a peregrine falcon nearly anywhere in North America, even around large cities. You'll need a sharp eye to see one on the move, unless it has been pulled over for a speeding ticket.

Learn more at distractfacts.com/fastfalcon.

BENNY CONTINUED HARASSING the barred owl but without Riley and Big Strig to help, his flight skills were no match. He tried to give chase as the owl broke free and sped away in the direction of the river.

Just ahead of the fleeing owl, the silhouette of two jet-black birds flying side-by-side materialized. "Oh no you don't!" shouted Harriet. She flew straight at the owl's face and Brock dive-bombed it from above, forcing it to turn back toward the rookery. Benny caught up and did his best to assist, but Harriet and Brock displayed their expert mobbing skills as they swooped back and forth at the owl, driving it anywhere they wished.

"We need to get it on the ground and make it talk!" Benny exclaimed.

"Easier said than done!" Brock replied. "We can force it to fly where we want but none of us are strong enough to take it down to the ground."

"Where is Big Strig?" cried Harriet as she made another sweeping pass inches above the owl's eyes.

"I don't know. He went to save Riley and they didn't make it back. I don't know what happened to them."

"What about Copper?" asked Brock as he zoomed by and swiped with his feet at the side of the barred owl. "She ran off, didn't she?"

Down on the ground, Copper had flattened herself in the weeds that covered the concrete pipe at the far end of the pond. She yearned for a couch to hide behind, but since there weren't any couches around the pond, the tall weeds provided the next best place for her to disappear. She couldn't see anything, and if she didn't sit up, she figured nothing could see her. Unfortunately, animals who hunt in the dark tend to notice things, like the shiny, silver ring on Copper's walking harness, when they are sticking up out of the weeds.

"Bet you never thought you'd be wishing to be back home with Yap," said a voice right behind her.

Copper vaulted into the air; if her tail had not been soaked to the bone, it would have reached maximum poof stage, roughly the size of a roll of paper towels. When she saw the hooked yellow bill and inky black eyes of her surprise visitor, her eyes popped open wide.

"Bart?"

"Yes?"

"How did you get behind me without me hearing you?"

"I'm an owl. We move silently. It's kind of our thing."

Did You Hear Something?

Owls have broad wings, so you'd expect to hear a whole lot of swooshing sounds when an owl flaps its humongous wings. Instead, owls have a specialized feather design which allows them to be as silent as mice in mime school.

What's the reason for the silent flight? One theory is that they need to be quiet when they are swooping down for a sneak attack on their prey. Another idea is based on the way owls use their amazing sense of hearing to locate prey. If their wings are noisily flapping, it might interfere with the ability to track a meal.

This answers the question pondered by philosophers for ages. If an owl flies through the woods and there is no one there to hear it, does it make a sound? No. No, it doesn't. Learn more at distractfacts.com/ninjaowl.

Copper backed away slowly from Bart. "Are you going to try to kill me again?"

"I haven't tried to kill you at all, as far as I know," said Bart. "I'd guess it was that barred owl Brock and Harriet are pushing around up there." He waved a wing at the sky. Copper glanced up just in time to see Harriet jab her bill into the side of the barred owl and turn it back toward Brock.

"Where did they come from? What are you doing here? Who is that owl? Why did it try to kill me?"

"That's a whole lot of questions and we don't have a whole lot of time," replied Bart. "Where's the great horned owl? I hate to say it, but we could kind of use him right now."

"I don't know. The last I saw him he had just pulled me out of the water and he was going back to get Riley off the other owl."

"Riley was *on* the other owl?" exclaimed Bart.

Hopping off the pipe, Copper landed near a bronze frog, who, of course, promptly squealed and dove into the water. Copper hissed. "Ohhhh, those things have been freaking me out all night. They're everywhere!" cried Copper. "Yes, Riley was on the other owl, somehow."

Bart gazed at the faint ripples rolling away from where the bronze frog had hit the water. Blinking in his usual slow manner, which looked as if he had to command his eyelids to open and close, the barred owl thought about the frog he'd just seen, one that was easily twice the size of Riley. Bart had an intense look on his face that Copper had already learned to recognize.

"Something on your mind?" she asked.

"Yeaaaah," he drawled. "Do you think you could run as fast as you can along the pond until I tell you to stop and then meet me back here on top of this pipe?"

That was the kind of question that required a Copper head-tilt.

"I suppose so. Why do you want me to do that?"

"No time to explain," Bart called as he took to the air. "Start running when I give the signal and then be ready when the moment comes!"

14

FROGS AWAY!

B art soared above Copper, swerving as a haggard black-crowned night heron swept by. It was struggling to keep up with Brock and Harriet. "Are you Benny?" Bart asked the heron.

"Yes," Benny panted. "Who are you?"

"My name is Bart. Harriet and Brock asked me to come here. They think I'm connected to all of this somehow, but they haven't had time to explain why. I want to help you find out what happened to your chicks. Are you ready to take this owl down?"

"Oh yeah, Bart. I'm more than ready to take this owl down. But I'm not adept at aerial combat. What do I need to do?"

"Stand on that pipe down there and wait for Copper to come back. She'll need your help."

"Gladly," said Benny as he peeled off and glided to a perch on top of the concrete pipe.

Bart watched as Harriet and Brock chased the barred owl toward the opposite end of the pond. "Harriet! Brock!" he shouted. "Bring the owl back this way and run it as low as you can!"

"Why?" yelled Brock.

"You got it!" shouted Harriet.

Bart stretched out his talons, clacked his beak, and took a deep breath. "Go now, Copper!" he cried.

Copper mustered every bit of strength she had left and ran like there was a fresh can of wet food waiting for her at the other end of the pond. As she ran, bronze frogs squeaked with every step and leapt into the pond. As Copper spooked frogs into the air, Bart dove for the water and raced behind her. He thought about his mama catching fish as he snatched one frog, then another into his talons. He grabbed a third frog in his beak and flapped up to Copper's ear.

"Rn bck nowf," he mumbled through a mouthful of frog and then shot up into the sky. Copper spun around without the slightest stumble and sprinted back to the pipe. High above the pond, Bart hovered with frogs at the ready as Brock and Harriet drove the other barred owl toward him. As they passed under him, Bart spiraled down, opened one talon like a bomb bay door, and released a frog.

"Eeeeeeep!" the frog called as it dropped onto its intended target. It landed squarely on the owl's back and clamped on like a bull-riding bronze frog. Bart had made a direct hit. As the weight of the hopping hitchhiker pushed the unidentified owl lower to the ground, Bart opened his second talon, bomb bay door number two.

"Eeeeeeep!" The second frog plunked the mystery owl in the head before tumbling backward and grabbing hold alongside the first. The double portion of croaking cargo on its back made the owl slow down and sink even lower to the ground.

Looking ahead, Bart saw Copper climbing the pipe at the end of the pond. He figured the other owl saw her too, which was why he had one more piece of amphibian ammunition to fire. With Brock and Harriet following close behind, Bart flew to the lead, lifted his head, and heaved the final frog directly into the other owl's face.

"Can't see! Can't see!" the owl screamed. With the frog stretched across its eyes, frog lips blocking one eye, and a frog butt over the other, the owl descended blindly and stretched its legs out to landing position.

"Take it down, Copper!" cried Bart as he veered to his left with Brock and Harriet.

The mysterious owl careened toward her with legs and wings flailing. Copper leapt into the air, wrapped it in a head-lock with her front legs, and slammed it down onto the concrete pipe. The owl fought Copper like a maniac. Mud and frogs flying in every direction, the ball of cat and owl bowled Benny over as the trio tumbled off the pipe.

Rolling to her side, Copper clutched the owl's head with her front legs and booted it in the ribs with her hind legs. Even though she outweighed it, she had to struggle to control the owl; she had never been in a fight before, and the ferocity of it shocked her.

Benny sprang back to his feet and jumped onto the owl's back. As it wheezed under his weight, Benny jabbed his heavy bill into its neck. "Stop fighting," Benny snarled. "You're not going anywhere, until you tell us what you did with my chicks."

Brock, Harriet, and Bart swooped down and gathered around the prisoner.

"Get off me, you despicable bird," the owl replied in a raspy, winded voice. "As usual, you're a tough guy when someone else has already done the work for you."

"What's that about?" Bart turned to Benny and asked, "Do you know this owl?"

The owl jerked its wings, attempting to free itself. Benny teetered, and Copper tightened her grip, digging her claws into the owl's neck.

"I don't have a clue who this is, Bart," said Benny as he regained his balance.

The captive owl suddenly stopped struggling. "What did you just call him?" it said.

"He called him Bart," answered Harriet. "Why? Do you know that name?"

The owl twisted its head in the mud to get a better look at Bart.

"Son?"

Bart leaned closer.

"Dad?"

"I thought you were dead!" the pair of barred owls cried in unison.

"I thought you were killed the night I lost your mama! Why are you working with one of the birds who attacked her?" exclaimed Bart's dad.

"What?" the entire group cried in unison.

"Ask him how he got that nice long scar on his bill," Bart's father grunted as he nodded toward Benny.

"I got this scar trying to help . . ." Benny's voice dropped to a whisper. "You were the one?"

"Yes, I was the one who slashed you when you and your great horned owl buddies tried to make a meal of my Belle."

"I wasn't attacking her; I was trying to help her!" Benny exclaimed.

"Why on earth would you be helping a creature you don't even know?"

"Because he has the choosing ability," Brock answered.

"Your son has it too," said Harriet, "and I think you have it as well."

"I don't understand what you're talking about," the owl replied. "Who are you?"

"Hey, anybody mind if we continue this conversation without me laying in the mud hugging an owl?" interrupted Copper.

Brock and Harriet looked at one another and then at Bart, who hadn't taken his eyes off his father. "Go ahead and let him loose, Copper," said Brock.

"We can't let him loose," Benny protested. "He hasn't—"

"He won't try to escape or fight," said Bart. "I think he needs to figure out what's going on as much as I do. If he leaves, he won't get any answers."

"You don't know that he won't try to escape! He's done

something with my chicks, and he tried to drown Copper in the pond."

"I didn't try to drown her," said Bart's dad. "How would I know she can't swim or fly? She has feathers. She's hanging around a pond in the middle of the night. When I got a better look at her, I didn't even know what kind of creature she was."

"I can see that," said Copper. "My appearance is a little . . . off tonight." She let go of him, rolled to her feet, and looked herself over. By this point, she had lost most of the black-crowned nestling feathers from her fur during the wrestling match with Bart's dad, but she had replaced them with barred owl feathers and a full-body mudpack.

Soooo much licking to do, she thought.

Benny squatted down, preparing for the owl to fight once Copper let go, but it didn't try to shake him off. Maybe Bart was right. Maybe they all needed to figure out things together. He stepped off the owl and faced the creature who had been taking his chicks.

"Okay, now that we are starting to become chums, we should introduce ourselves," said Harriet. "I'm Harriet, my sometimes cranky but always loveable companion here is Brock, and the fellow who just got off your back is Benny. We are members of the FLOCC. You obviously already know Bart. The mystery creature who tackled you is Copper; she's a house cat."

"That's a house cat?" asked the owl. "I've heard of them, but I didn't know they looked so . . . different."

"Like I said, it's a bad fur day for me," replied Copper. "Cut me some slack, owl."

"You just tackled me and kicked me in the side about twenty times. You're lucky I don't come over there and pluck your feathers."

"Go ahead and try it, buddy." Copper swatted the air a few times with her paw. "We'll see how you like another round of this."

"Knock it off!" cried Brock. "Now that you know who we are, what is your name?"

"My name is Elliott, but Bart calls me Dad." Elliott turned to Bart. "Where have you been, son? I've been all alone in our woods."

"I'm sorry, Dad. I didn't know. I tried to follow you and fight that night, but I was too slow. A second great horned owl flew in to join the one that attacked mama, and I panicked. There was so much screeching—I just flew away to hide. I never went back because I thought they had killed you, too. I never imagined that you could defeat one great horned owl on your own, much less two."

"I didn't defeat them. When I got to her, she was already—" Elliott stopped and looked to the sky. "She was dangling life-lessly in the grasp of a great horned owl. This cowardly character"—he shook a wing at Benny—"was flying around trying to steal from the owl and take an easy meal for himself. I charged in and got a good slash on him with my talons. That's where he picked up that little souvenir across his bill. He flew away once he realized he was in for a real fight."

Bart turned to look at Benny and the black-crowned night heron was shaking his head. "No, not true," the heron said.

"I chased after the great horned owl carrying your mama," Elliott continued, "and that's when the second one rushed by me. I figured it was going to attack, but it seemed to have no interest in me. Both owls disappeared into the forest, and that was the moment I realized I didn't know where you were. I hurried back to our tree hollow, but I couldn't find you anywhere. I thought they had taken you as well."

Bart trembled as the memories of that horrible night flipped through his mind. He turned back to Benny. "Is this true? Were you there that night?"

"I was there, but that's not what happened," answered Benny. "I was trying to help your mama."

"Nonsense!" shouted Elliott. "I know what I saw. I've replayed that scene in my head many times over the last year, as I sat alone in our woods. All I've been able to do is think about what I should have done differently. I should have been more alert and sensed the great horned owls were nearby. I should have told Bart to hide in the tree hollow instead of drawing him out to the fight. I should have taken the opportunity to kill the great horned owl when it was preoccupied with this scavenging black-crowned night heron. At least that would have given me the satisfaction of avenging Belle's death."

"But I can see that you're a creature with the choosing ability," interrupted Harriet. "You would not have felt satisfaction with revenge. You would still hurt."

"So what," said Elliot. "I haven't even wanted to exist since that night. Most days I've only sat there with these overwhelming feelings of sadness and loneliness clouding my mind. I'd see other animals in the forest, going about their business, and I wanted them to feel like me. I wanted them to be sad. It was weird. I don't know how to describe it."

Harriet nodded. "You don't have to explain that feeling. I believe all of us here know what you're talking about in some way. But how did you end up here?"

Benny flinched as Elliott stepped toward him. He could see his face reflecting in the owl's angry black eyes. "Because this guy had the nerve to come back to my woods this spring," said Elliott. "I couldn't believe my eyes when I saw the same black-crowned night heron with the scar I gave him. He was foraging with his mate in the creek below our empty tree hole, mocking me."

"We weren't mocking you," growled Benny. "Betty and I have foraged in that creek every spring for years. We didn't even know you were there."

"I know you didn't know I was there. I could have easily attacked you both before you knew what hit you. That's what I wanted to do, but I kept fighting with myself in my head. Some sense I couldn't explain was telling me not to do it. Before I could sort out my thoughts, you took off. I followed you all the way back to your rookery."

"How did they not know you were following them?" asked Copper.

"I'm an owl. We move silently. It's kind of our thing," replied Elliott.

Bart looked at Copper, giving her an "I told you so" shoulder shrug.

"I saw that they were bringing food back for their chicks," Elliott continued. "There they were, foraging together in my woods, right below my empty tree hollow, and bringing food back to their nice, happy nest. I couldn't stand it. Then, I saw their oldest chick leave the nest. It couldn't fly yet, but it joined a group of other chicks and began to feed in this pond. None of the adults were with them. And an idea entered my mind. I could give that black-crowned night heron a taste of my hurt. I would take his chicks and make him feel the agony of coming home to an empty nest. I started to get that sense again of fighting myself in my mind. But I felt that I had failed my family, and this was a way for me do something to make it up. So, I shut everything else out and I plucked his chick right out of the group."

Benny wailed, and Harriet wrapped a wing around him.

"I'll bet you didn't feel better after that though, did you?" asked Brock.

Elliott scowled at Brock. "No, but I figured that was because I knew he had more chicks. They all needed to go. I came back night after night, and as they left the nest and foraged along the pond, I snatched them up."

"But if you were trying to hurt Benny, why did you take one of the other night heron's chicks?" asked Copper.

"That was a mistake. I had to change my hunting position to this end of the pond because I noticed a great horned owl hiding in the trees last night. I thought the chick had left the same nest as all the others, but it must have been from a different nest in the same tree. I didn't realize it until I came back tonight and saw *he* still had a chick."

Benny began bawling so loudly that all the animals besides Harriet stepped back. It occurred to Copper that her first time hearing a black-crowned night heron laugh and cry had happened on the same night. She liked the laughter much better.

"You've piled one mistake on top of another in this," Benny blubbered. "I was never trying to hurt your mate, and nothing you have done will make you feel better. Is that why you came back tonight? You wanted to see my pain, thinking yours would be gone?"

"Yes."

"Well, you were wrong," said Harriet. "I think you know that in your heart."

Benny stood tall, causing Harriet's wing to slip from his back. "I guess you've succeeded in part of your mission though," he said. "You have made me feel your hurt. I'm sorry for what happened to Belle, but I was trying to help her that night. I've lost my children, and my mate is going to leave me. I'll be alone and sad, like you were, but nothing will have improved in your life because of it."

"You won't be alone, Benny," said Brock. "The FLOCC will be here to help you. I only wish we had known about Elliott before all of this happened. Maybe we could have helped him."

Elliott scoffed at Brock. "You all keep talking about helping other creatures. Even if I believed that this black-crowned night heron was trying to help Belle, what good did it do? Suppose by some miracle, he fought off the owl who attacked her. There was another one right behind it, ready to do the same thing. The world is hard."

Bart had an intense look on his face that everyone was getting used to seeing. There was something on his mind.

"Dad, if we have an opportunity to do something good, to help another creature, why wouldn't we? You're right about the world being hard. I've seen it close and personal, just like you. Things will always be hard. That's natural life. If I have the choosing ability, and I choose to do something that helps others, then I have made the world a little better. If enough creatures with the choosing ability do the same, I'm thinking we'll have a much better world for everyone."

Harriet caught Brock's eye and held up her wings as if she had scored the winning goal in the big game. He gave a mock bow to recognize the triumph of her intuition about Bart.

"Bart has said it well," said Brock. "Each act of kindness leads to another. It's like the trees in your forest. When they were small seedlings and saplings, they weren't much good to the owls who lived there at that time. Your life is better because, little by little, those trees grew into the big, beautiful forest you have now. We want to be the seedlings of a great big forest of creatures who care, one that covers the world."

"Sounds great," said Elliott, "but that world doesn't exist right now. If I had helped a thousand creatures, Belle still wouldn't be here with us. The hard things of this world are forest fires blazing through all the seedlings before your forest of *caring* ever gets a chance to grow. You're so busy thinking about making some future caring world, you aren't prepared to deal with the one you live in."

"Aren't prepared?" argued Brock. "That's one of the main reasons the FLOCC exists. You mentioned fire. In some of the forests around here, there is a type of tree we call the longleaf pine. Do you know it?"

"Of course, I do. Those are some of the tallest pines with the longest needles in the forest. What does that have to do with anything?"

"I've seen a forest after a fire, and those trees seemed to survive the fire more than other types of trees. I don't know why, but maybe there's something special about the bark. The trees might have been scorched and the needles burned, but the trees continued to thrive. One member of the FLOCC is like one of those trees, and all the other members are like those special pieces of bark. Fire will come, but we support each other so that our little forest continues to grow. We don't want the fire, but together, we're ready for it. Just like we were ready for you tonight."

That's One Fine Pine
Trees and fire don't normally mix, but the longleaf pine (*Pinus palustris*) is a different kind of tree in many ways. For one thing, it spends its first few years growing down instead of up! During those early years, most of its energy

goes into growing a main root, called the taproot, which can end up being nearly as wide as the tree's trunk. That strong anchor helps the tree reach its full potential, which can be 100 feet tall and over 200 years old.

The taproot isn't the only thing that makes these trees tough. The bark on a longleaf pine helps it to be fire-resistant, which allows it to thrive even when periodic lightning fires or controlled burns thin out the forest understory. Longleafs are also more resistant to beetle attacks, and they can handle floods and droughts better than other types of trees.

Longleaf pine forests are mostly found in the southeastern United States, and a lot of unique plants and animals live in those forests. Protected animals like red-cockaded woodpeckers and gopher tortoises prefer to make their homes in longleaf pine forests. Along with the animals, you'll also find special plants called pitcher plants hanging out around the longleaf pines. These are plants that trap and eat insects! There is no need to plug up your bug zapper when you've got pitcher plants hanging around.

Learn more at distractfacts.com/finepine.

"LOOK AROUND YOU, ELLIOTT," said Harriet. "There's a house cat, a couple of crows, and even your son out here helping a black-crowned night heron. Somewhere around here a tree frog and a great horned owl are helping as well. All of us are here to help another creature. None of these animals has anything to gain by helping Benny. We're here to help him through one of those fires like Brock just described."

"Don't forget, the human is also helping us. I wouldn't be here if it weren't for him," added Copper.

"You've got a human helping? They can have the choosing ability as well?" asked Elliott.

"I have my doubts," said Brock. "He helps us, but that doesn't mean he has the choosing ability. It may simply be something he does naturally for his survival. We just don't know enough about humans yet."

"Brock always has his doubts," said Harriet. "It's good because he's protective over the FLOCC, but it can be a bit annoying at times."

"Which times?" said Bart. "Morning, noon, and night?"

The hodgepodge of tired, ragged animals all had a laugh. Even Benny managed a chuckle, but then a handful of black-crowned night herons flew by, which brought him back to the terrible reality of his situation.

"The scouts are back already! I need to go back and see Betty one last time before she leaves me. I don't think it will be long now."

"Why is she leaving you?" asked Elliott.

Benny glared at the barred owl. "Because you killed our chicks," he said with a fierceness that matched his fiery-red eyes. "The whole colony thinks I'm the one who brought the danger here! They're all leaving me."

Seeing his son cringe at the sting in Benny's words, Elliott hung his head. "I didn't kill your chicks," he muttered. "I didn't want to hurt them at all. I just got it in my head that I could make myself feel better by watching you suffer, even for a little while. I was going to bring them back."

"Bring them back from where?" cried Benny.

"Just across the river. There's another black-crowned night heron rookery by the water. It's the place where the humans are always walking around. I've been checking on them. The herons over there are taking care of them as if they were their own."

Found a Sitter!
Black-crowned night herons are all one big happy family when it comes to taking care of the little ones. Parents will look after any chicks that appear in their nest, not just their own. One theory is that the parents can't tell the difference between their own chicks and those of others.

This habit is especially helpful when a black-crowned night heron couple wants to go to the movies. They simply slide their chicks into the nest next door and it's off to the theater!

Learn more at distractfacts.com/movienight.

"I KNOW THAT PLACE," said Harriet. "We've scavenged the cans there before. Humans put perfectly good food in them for some reason."

"Dad, you can still put this right," said Bart. "We need to get those chicks. Maybe Benny can convince Betty and everyone else to stay, once they see the chicks are safe."

"There are five of them and only Bart and Elliott have the strength to carry a chick," said Brock. "Benny isn't built for carrying that kind of weight in flight. That means at least three trips across the river, unless we can get Big Strig involved. It's going to take a few hours."

"I don't think we'll have that much time," said Benny. "The scouts will get everyone moving as soon as they can because we prefer to fly at night and lay low during the day. It won't be long before daylight."

"But what about the birds who can't fly yet, like Steve?" asked Copper. "How will they get to the new colony?"

"They won't get to the new colony," said Benny. "When a colony is abandoned, everything gets left behind."

"That's awful!" exclaimed Copper. "Then what can we do to save the colony?"

"We're going to have to come up with something faster than owl transport to get those chicks over here," said Harriet. "I think I may have an idea, but we need the human and we have to have Riley as well. Brock, you and I should fly to the other rookery. Benny, do what you can to delay the colony. The rest of you, find Big Strig and Riley."

Harriet didn't wait for a reply. She and Brock rocketed across the river. Benny ran for his nest as fast as his stubby legs would carry him, leaving Elliott, Bart, and Copper standing together in the mud.

"So, who's Riley?" asked Elliott.

15

TIME TOW CAW A TAXI

Kyle stood at the resort office door and scanned the parking lot. He had assumed the animals were still waiting in his tow truck, but Julius Swine's story had him worried. Swine had rushed into the office in a state of panic after his toilet-unclogging operation. Soaking wet, the manager had slammed the door and awakened Kyle from his little catnap. Kyle had thought it must have been the worst clogged toilet of all time.

Swine had ripped off his shirt and thrown it on the floor, while he rambled on about birds throwing things at him and trying to ambush him. Then he had taken a letter opener off the desk and flipped the shirt repeatedly, searching for something he had felt on his back. Each time he flipped the shirt over, he would jump away and point the letter opener at it, like he was expecting a deadly cobra hidden in there.

The last thing anyone needs to see as soon as they are jolted from a good sleep is a shirtless Julius Swine, dripping with rain and thrashing around at an invisible cobra. It was like watching a sea lion wearing a furry cape while operating a jackhammer. Swine's naturally bed-heady hair was even more tousled than it had been earlier. Kyle figured a bird could easily make a nest in there without Swine even knowing it.

After half a dozen shirt flips, several trips to the water cooler, and a visit to the restroom, Swine had finally calmed down enough to tell Kyle what had happened in the parking lot: the horrible screeching of birds fighting in the rookery, the strange rustling of animals in the bushes, and the alarming squealing of frogs.

"Then they threw something at me," bellowed Swine.

"They?" asked Kyle. He had been looking out the door as Swine told his story, not only to watch the parking lot, but also to avoid looking at the still-shirtless Swine. Kyle gulped and turned back to face the resort owner.

"They . . . the birds," replied Swine. "At least, I think it was the birds. They were too high up to be anything else. They missed me with the first one and hit the streetlight above my head. Whatever they threw was heavy because I heard it hit the ground hard. The second one got me in the back. Did it leave a mark?" He turned his hairy back to Kyle, causing him to nearly heave.

If there was a mark on Swine's back, finding it would be like spotting a caterpillar in an aerial photo of a rainforest. "No, I'm not seeing a mark," Kyle said as he averted his eyes to the ceiling, and that's when he noticed something even more odd than Julius Swine's back.

There was a green tree frog sitting in the tangled nest of hair atop Swine's head.

Kyle's jaw dropped. *Is that the same frog from the truck?*

The frog gave a long-toed wave to Kyle. Yep, it was the frog from the truck.

Swine turned around again, and the tree frog twisted with

him. Kyle tried not to look at the frog so that he wouldn't draw Swine's attention to it.

"Well, I definitely felt something hit me," said Swine. "I don't know what it was, and I didn't stick around to find out. I think those crazy birds must know I don't like them. That's the only reason they would throw things at me."

"Uh, yeah," said Kyle as he struggled to keep his eyes from flittering up to the frog. "Maybe so. I think animals are a lot more aware of things than we give them credit for."

"Probably right," said Swine. "Is there something bothering you?"

"What? Why do you say that?"

"It seems like your eyes are freaking out or something."

"Oh, no, I'm just realizing that I left my truck running and I need to go check on it." Kyle awkwardly motioned toward the parking lot a couple of times. "I'm going to go check on my truck. You might want to grab a shirt in case a visitor pops in."

"Oh! Sorry about that. I didn't even think about it since I was all worked up about the bird attack. Fortunately, I've got some spare resort shirts in the back." Swine twirled around, and the frog did likewise.

Taking off his baseball cap, Kyle pointed at it, hoping the frog would get the idea. The frog double-jumped onto the desk and right into Kyle's hat just as Swine brushed at the back of his head.

Without missing a beat, Kyle flipped the hat on and scooted out the door with a frog on his head and a pep in his step. Hurrying across the parking lot, Kyle noticed two barred owls walking on either side of a wobbly-looking great horned owl. It had a wing on each barred owl's back, as if they were helping it stay upright. Another animal that resembled a soggy cat wearing a feather-adorned ninja suit ambled along behind them.

"What on earth?" exclaimed Kyle as the bizarre ensemble joined him at the tow truck. He opened his door and water poured onto the pavement. "Who put my window all the way down? My seat is soaking wet!" he cried.

None of the animals confessed to the window-lowering. The feathery ninja cat jumped into the cab, sprawled out on the floormat, and began licking at its tail like a kid with a melty ice cream cone.

"I guess we'll wait in there for Harriet and Brock," said Bart. "Big Strig, you're going to have to get in on your own. We don't have a way to lift you up there."

"I's canns handle ut," Big Strig slurred.

Kyle listened to the owls carry on a conversation with one of the barred owls hooting and the great horned owl making a gurgling sound. Then the barred owls flapped into the cab, but the great horned owl missed the open door by three feet and bonked into the side of the truck.

"You look a little out of it, big guy," said Kyle. "Mind if I help?" He held out his hands like he was trying to show the owl he was unarmed. Once he was confident the owl would not try to rip out his eyeballs, Kyle hoisted it into the truck. Grabbing a rag from behind the seat, Kyle dried a spot off for himself and slid in next to his ever-growing group of passengers. "I'd sure love to know what y'all have been up to," he said as he tipped his cap to let the tree frog out on the dashboard.

"How is Strig?" asked Riley. "Is he okay?"

"I think he's okay, but he's a little loopy," answered Bart. "We found him staggering around outside the pond. What happened?"

"I think he got knocked out. We crashed into one of those lights after he rescued me from the"—Riley suddenly noticed the second barred owl in the truck—"from him! What's he doing here?"

"Riley, meet my dad, Elliott. Dad, this is Riley. You may be the only creature around who doesn't know Riley."

"Now that I see him, I realize we have met before," said Elliott. "He stuck his butt on my eye a little while ago."

"Ah, well that makes sense. Wait—"

"I've actually seen you before tonight," Riley interrupted, "but we didn't officially meet."

"When was that?" asked Elliott.

"When Bart came to FLOCC headquarters earlier, he shared his story of the night he lost his mom. We recognized a lot of the details, because Strig and I were there that night too."

"What were you doing there?" Elliot exclaimed.

"We had a report of a female barred owl in that part of the

forest that had shown signs of the choosing ability. Strig and I were there to scout her out. We saw everything that happened. I'm sorry you lost your mate."

"If you were there, why didn't you try to help us?" asked Bart.

"We did try to help. Strig was on the move as soon as we saw the attack. We also saw Benny trying to help, which was the first clue for us that *he* had the choosing ability. Unfortunately, your dad was confused and went after Benny first. That gave the owl who attacked your mom an opportunity to get away. Strig chased the attacker down and forced it to let her go, but he was too late."

"So, he was the second great horned owl," Elliott said softly. "He was trying to help, too."

Kyle listened to the owls and frog chattering away at one another. *They're at it again*, he thought. *Wish I knew what they were saying.* The cat was too busy self-cleaning the crud off its tail to participate in the chat. It had cleared away one tiny patch of orange-stripy fur, which confirmed the filthy cat was the same one he had left in the truck.

"Yes," Riley confirmed to Elliott. "After Bart told us his story, we knew there was a connection between him and Benny. That's why Harriet and Brock went to find Bart after the sentinels chased him away from headquarters. Honestly, we began to suspect he might have been the one targeting Benny."

Bart threw up his wings. "You thought it was me? Is that why Harriet and Brock asked me to follow them to the rookery? To confront me with Benny?"

"Maybe so," said Riley, "but how did you end up catching your dad?"

"I only helped. Copper is the one who caught him."

"Way to go, Copper!" cheered Riley. "I knew you'd be great at this!"

"Can't talk. Cleaning," she replied between licks.

"What about Benny's chicks?" asked Riley.

"They're all okay," said Bart. "Dad had taken them to another rookery across the river, thinking that was a way to get back at Benny. We need to bring them back and, hopefully, everything will then be fine. Brock and Harriet are working on a plan to use the human to help us."

Riley did a celebratory hop on the dashboard. "Yes! That's awesome! Where are Brock and Harriet now?"

Kyle screamed like a pig riding a roller coaster when two black crows whooshed into the truck and landed next to the frog on the dashboard. It was the pair from the junkyard, and one of them dropped a damp piece of paper onto the floor.

"Hopefully this will work," Harriet puffed. "It looks a little different from the tokens we give him that he calls 'photo.' We had to take the first thing we could find, and there was a stack of these in the cans near the rookery."

"What did you bring me this time?" Kyle picked up the paper and noticed his hands were shaking. Those birds had nearly caused him to need a new pair of underwear. "Hmm, it's the daily dinner specials from Oyster Point Bed & Breakfast," said Kyle. "You two looking to go on a date night?" He grinned as he looked at the crow couple, and then back to the other animals in the truck. The only sound was from the cat slurping at her tail. It was halfway clean already.

"Tough crowd," said Kyle. "I'm not familiar with this place, but it says it's on South Battery Street. Should be near White Point Garden. Probably a ten minute drive this time of night." He yawned and shifted the truck into gear. "I guess I might as well check it out since we've come this far together. Y'all need to start chipping in some gas money, though!"

Noticing that the truck started moving, Bart asked, "Does that mean the token worked?"

"I'm not sure," replied Brock. "We'll find out soon enough."

The rain had subsided, so Kyle lowered the windows to air out the truck. Between the wet seat and some funky-smelling animals, the air was a bit stale in the cab, but he was relieved that at least the goat wasn't there, too. As the truck accelerated across the Ravenel Bridge, the roar of wind and engine was nearly drowned out by the chatter of the animals.

"So where were you and Big Strig while we were having all the fun with Bart's dad?" Harriet asked Riley.

"Ha! Strig and I had softened him up before you came in and got the easy capture."

Copper took a break from her maniacal cleaning routine. "Easy capture? Try catching an angry owl in midair and let me know if you still think it's easy."

"I wouldn't call it midair," said Elliott. "If my son hadn't loaded me down with frogs, your wingless self would have grabbed nothing but a meandering moth."

"Loaded you down with frogs?" questioned Riley.

"Had to use the resources that were available, you know?" said Bart.

Kyle slowed the truck as a cat scampered across the street near a row of historic houses, each painted a different shade, like a vibrant pastel rainbow. Light from oil lamps flickered across his hood as he drove on, and the waterfront shimmered ahead as they approached the area known as the Battery, where a seawall with a walkway along the top guarded the shores of the Charleston peninsula. Kyle turned down a street that ran parallel to White Point Garden, a beautiful park where the spreading branches of old live oak trees sheltered historical monuments, Civil War cannons, and walking paths.

Opposite the park, two brick columns guarded a narrow cobblestone driveway that curved behind one of the many historical homes lining the street. The house was three-stories tall with porches across the front on every level. Even in the pre-dawn darkness, it gleamed white, like the feathers of a snowy egret. A weathered sign nailed to one of the columns read "Oyster Point Bed & Breakfast."

"This is the place," announced Kyle. "Now what do we do?"

"This is the place," said Harriet. She swung a wing at the park. "The black-crowned night herons nest in those trees over there. We need to quickly find out where the chicks are. Riley, do you happen to know any of the night herons here?"

"As a matter of fact, I do," Riley replied with a big smile on his face. "I'm going to need a lift, though. My usual ride is out of commission right now."

"I'm feeling better," said Big Strig. "My head feels like there's a woodpecker inside my skull, but I should be able to fly straight. I think."

"Let me take you," offered Elliott.

"I don't think that's a good idea," argued Big Strig.

"I think it's a wonderful idea," said Harriet. "We're here because Elliott made some bad choices, but now he's trying to make it right. None of us with the choosing ability makes the right choice every time, but we can always make a good choice the next time."

"I'm fine with it," said Riley. "Elliot didn't have to tell anyone where the chicks were. Like Harriet pointed out, he obviously wants to make this right. Just don't squeeze too tight, big fella. The only thing busting guts around here should be my jokes."

"No problem," said Elliott.

Kyle jerked his head back as one of the barred owls hopped onto the dashboard, wrapped its talons around the tree frog, and flapped out of the window. He watched as the owl and the frog landed in one of the trees in the park. After a few minutes of night heron KWAKing, frog peeping, and a couple of owl hoots, a handful of adult black-crowned night herons glided down, their white bellies and silver wings looking ghostly in the dim lights that illuminated the park. Several brown juveniles were foraging in the shrubbery around one of the monuments, and the adults herded them toward the tow truck.

After the owl and the frog returned from the tree, they stood on the curb alongside the juvenile black-crowned night herons, all staring at Kyle. Unsure of what to do next, Kyle just opened his door and then one of the adult herons made several clucking sounds. One-by-one, five young night herons hopped into his tow truck, followed by the owl and the frog. "You two coming?" Kyle said to the pair of adult herons who had herded the young ones over.

"What did he say?" one of the night herons asked the other.

"I have no clue what those human noises mean," he replied. "But they do leave good food in the cans."

As the pair of night herons KWAKed and flew back to the trees, Kyle decided that their response was a definite no. When he started to get back in his tow truck, he realized there was one more thing he needed to do. Kyle pulled out his phone and took a photo of himself with two American crows, two barred owls, five black-crowned night heron chicks, a great horned owl, a tree frog, and a disgusting-looking cat with a half-cleaned tail, all gathered in the truck behind him. He would never need a picture to remember this moment, but he knew the photo would bring an instant smile any time he looked at it in the future.

"What's he doing?" asked Bart.

"I don't know, but my humans do that all the time," said Copper. "They make weird faces and strange hand gestures while they're doing it. Then they start tapping on that thing like crazy and putting it down and picking it up over and over again. It doesn't seem natural. I think it must have catnip in it."

"We have a lot to learn about humans," said Brock. "I feel like we're making a little progress with this one, but how can we get him to take us back to Benny? We don't have a token to give him."

"How did you get him to go there in the first place?" asked Bart.

Brock motioned toward the Hog Island Resort brochure on the floorboard. "We gave him that token down there. Since we've been working with him, we figured out that one of the things he understands is tokens that look like the places we need to go. He makes a sound like 'photo' whenever we show him one."

"Why don't you try to present him the same token again?" suggested Bart.

"Might as well give it a try," said Harriet. "We've always given him a new token each time, but who knows? It might work."

Kyle climbed back into the truck and Brock hopped to the floor. He pecked on the Hog Island Resort brochure, which rested underneath the plunger cup.

"You want me to unclog a toilet?" asked Kyle.

None of the animals made a sound, but they all seemed to be looking back and forth at each other. The crow pecked a few more times at the brochure.

"Are you wanting to go back to the resort? The place in the photo?"

"Yes, he got it!" Harriet cried.

Every animal in the truck called out at the same time. The owls hooted, the crows cawed, the cat meowed, the frog sang, and it even looked like the two barred owls did a high five with their wings. Kyle figured that was a good sign that he had correctly guessed the destination.

16

THE RETURN OF STEVE

Quiet returned to the truck as Kyle drove the streets of downtown Charleston with an exotic petting zoo riding along. The cat was licking at its tail again, making steady progress, but the rest of the animals seemed to be lost in thought. As the truck merged onto the towering bridge for the third time that evening, Kyle turned on the radio.

"Good morning, Charleston," announced the voice on the radio. "That rainstorm we had overnight was quite the toad-strangler, folks. Are you wondering if it's going to rain as you're out and about later today? We'll all find out together at the top of the hour when Charleston's Wizard of Weather, Bill Fowler, joins us live in studio for his Famous First Flip Forecast. As Bill loves to say, he flips a coin, so you don't have to."

The announcer's voice faded into the sounds of Johnny Jones Johnson Junior's twangy guitar and Kyle cranked up the volume for another performance of "No Truck, No Lady, No Dog with Me." Big Strig jumped to the dashboard and promptly pecked the radio off. Apparently, the great horned owl was feeling better. The tow truck once again pulled into the parking lot at the Hog Island Resort, and Kyle parked in the same spot beside the walking path. A few black-crowned night herons settled into the trees, returning from their nighttime forage. He looked at the five chicks huddled on the floorboard next to the cat. "Hmm," he said, "I guess the cat wasn't the only animal who needed to get home tonight. Awesome! I sure hope I don't run into Mr. Swine again. This would be a little weird to explain."

He opened the door and a dozen animals flapped, hopped, and sauntered out of the truck onto the parking lot. As feet hit the pavement, something stirred in the dense foliage overhanging the railing on the adjacent walking path. Two black-crowned night herons popped out of the bushes.

"See, Betty, I told you they were all okay!" Benny exclaimed as Bonnie, Brady, Brody, and Bailey ran to greet their mom and dad. "Hey Nick, come see who just arrived!"

A second pair of adults jumped out from the bushes and the last chick dashed over to them. "Thanks," Nick squawked at Benny and disappeared into the bushes with his mate and his young one by his side.

"Good old Nick," said Benny. "Always a witty conversationalist."

Elliott shuffled over to face Benny and Betty. "I want to apologize for what I've done," he said. "I realize I was wrong when I thought you were trying to hurt Belle, and I was wrong in how I handled it."

"I forgive you," said Benny. "I'm grateful you helped to make things right, and I think everything is going to be okay. The last of the adults got back from foraging a few moments ago, and the first thing they'll all talk about is whether they need to abandon the colony today. Since the chicks are all here now, I don't think the other night herons will be fearful any longer, so they won't have a reason to leave the rookery. Because we have chicks wandering into other nests all the time, it's like they were never really gone." He leaned his head into Betty. "I know Betty is happy, so no matter what, I'm happy."

"Elliott, now that you know you have the choosing ability, we would love to get to know you better. Maybe get you involved with the FLOCC," said Harriet.

"That sounds pretty good, but I need to take some time to think things through." Elliot turned to Bart. "Will you come and visit me sometime soon at our old tree hollow?"

"Absolutely," Bart replied. "Now that I know no great horned owls are lurking around there, it's finally worth a trip home."

Big Strig hissed. "You know we aren't all bad, right?"

Bart shrugged his shoulders. "All the ones I've ever dealt with are . . . up until tonight, anyway."

"Strig is the only great horned owl we've come across who has the choosing ability," said Riley. "The others aren't good or bad, they're simply acting naturally. If there is another who has the choosing ability, I hope we get to them quickly. Predators with that much power who don't think about other creatures could do some serious damage to all of us, including themselves."

"True enough," said Bart, "but please forgive me if I enjoy antagonizing Mr. Toilet Beak here at future FLOCC meetings."

"Toilet beak?" asked Benny. "What does that mean?"

"It doesn't mean anything!" Big Strig growled. "Besides, who said Bart would be involved in FLOCC meetings anyway? None of us even knew he existed before tonight."

"I think he has proven that he has the choosing ability and

he cares about other creatures," said Riley. "Plus, I get the feeling that he'll keep nosing in on our missions anyway, so we might as well make him an official member of our squad."

"We have the whole leadership team here, so why don't we put it to a vote?" asked Harriet.

"Not the whole leadership team," said Big Strig. "We're missing Sarge."

"Yes, and on that topic," said Harriet, "even though some of us"—she shot a look at Brock—"weren't too sure about Copper's abilities, Sarge was confident. He said she would prove herself, in her own crazy way. He has already given his vote for Copper to join the FLOCC if she wants."

Copper perked her ears and sat tall on the sidewalk. She purred loudly enough to drown out the southern toads.

Harriet glanced at Riley, who nodded, and then she looked to Brock.

Brock sighed and stepped closer to Copper. "Sarge has believed in you since you were a kitten. I've known him a long time and I trust him completely, but that's because we've been through many trials and tests together. I feel that creatures need to earn trust before it is given to them. When you arrived at our headquarters, I wasn't convinced that you truly cared about other creatures. You could have been there merely for the thrill of an adventure. But an animal's true nature is revealed when it faces adversity, and you put yourself in danger tonight to help Benny, a creature you had never met and had no self-serving reason to help. You were brave."

"Thank you," said Copper, "but I don't know how brave I was. I've been scared almost the entire night. I've wanted to hide a lot."

"Being brave doesn't mean you aren't scared," said Riley. "In fact, to be brave you have to fear something in the first place. Bravery means you chose to do the right thing even though you were scared."

"And your bravery and self-sacrifice tonight prove that Sarge was right about you. I would be honored to serve by your side on the FLOCC leadership team," added Brock.

"Did you say . . . leadership team?" asked Copper with an extra-strength head-tilt.

"Yes, he did," said Riley. "Sarge not only thinks you should be in the FLOCC, he wants you to take over his spot on the leadership team."

"But where is he going? Why would he step down from the leadership team?"

"He wants to focus on finding more house animals with the choosing ability," Riley replied. "Sarge believes strongly that we need to learn more about humans. Since FLOCC leaders are generally involved in all our missions, it pulls him away from tracking down potential house animals."

"I see. If the leaders are involved in all the missions, does that mean I can't go back home if I become a FLOCC leader?"

"No, quite the opposite in fact," answered Brock. "The whole idea behind our House Animal Project is to learn more about humans. You have access to humans that none of us out here have. You can study them, learn how they interact and communicate with each other, and help us to figure out how to tell if any of them has the choosing ability."

"If any have the choosing ability, are those the ones who can help us on our missions?" asked Copper.

"Yes, but that's only part of it," said Harriet. "We already know they can help us, but if we learn more about them, we might find ways that we can help them, too. Humans do a lot of strange things. If you ask us crows, so do frogs, owls, cats, night herons, and all other creatures. We all share the same world though, so I'm pretty sure helping them is good for all of us."

"Which means we need you at home, studying those humans for us," said Riley. "You might have noticed that when it's time for a mission, we have our ways of getting you involved." He took one of his front legs and waved his padded toes around his bulging eyes. "Just think. If you accept, you get to see a lot more of this handsome face."

Copper laughed. "I don't know, Riley, I was leaning toward accepting until you threatened me with that. Look how grumpy all that frog face time has made Big Strig."

"I'm not grumpy," Big Strig grumbled. "My job requires intense concentration. I have to protect everyone and watch out for danger, like that bird that's sneaking up behind you."

Copper whirled around, and as she did so, her tail

smacked the face of another young black-crowned night heron who had come wobbling out from the bushes. The youngster did what most chicks like him do when they're scared.

He vomited. All over Copper's tail.

"Everyone, I'd like to introduce you to my youngest chick, Steve," said Benny. "Copper, I believe you two have met before."

"You have GOT to be kidding me!" Copper cried. "I just got done cleaning that!"

On a night filled with many firsts, Copper added one more to her list as she heard a group of many different animals all laughing together. Even the human was making a sound like laughter. *That's a sweet sound*, thought Copper as she joined in the laughter. *I could get used to this, even if it means a little more cleaning to do.*

"Okay. I'm in," Copper announced, "and as my first act of leadership, I do hereby cast my vote to accept Bart the barred owl as a new member of the FLOCC."

"And, although I'd still like to know more about that frog dropping thing, I'm also a yes for Bart joining us," said Riley.

"The vote is a no-brainer for me as well," added Harriet. "Definitely a yes."

"We've known about Copper for a while, but we just met Bart," said Brock. "He has shown he has the choosing ability, and he acted selfless and brave like Copper tonight, but I'd like to get to know him better."

Bart looked to Copper, puffed out his feathers, and swiped a wing across his face.

"And the best way to get to know him," Brock continued, "will be to have him as part of our team. Welcome to the FLOCC, Bart."

"Yes!" exclaimed Bart. He bent down, and Copper head-butted him so hard he nearly toppled over.

"What about the human?" asked Benny. "He did a lot of things for us tonight. I think he has the choosing ability and has chosen to help other creatures. Shouldn't he be an official member of the FLOCC as well?"

"I think you're right Benny," Riley agreed. "He's shown us everything we look for in a FLOCC member. As an added bonus, he hasn't tried to eat me yet! My vote is yes for the human."

Copper brushed a paw against her nose. "He took that pipe off my face earlier," said Copper. "If he hadn't done anything else the rest of the night, he'd have my vote!"

"He would be the first human member of a FLOCC squad, as far as I know," said Harriet. "If there are others who have the choosing ability, I can't wait to find them. We'll be able to do some incredible things with humans like this one working with us. He obviously cares about other creatures, and I think he's the perfect choice for our first FLOCC human member."

"I still have my doubts about him, but he's been a tremendous helper," said Brock. "There isn't much risk in making him an official member. I'm not even sure how he'll know he's part of the FLOCC."

Copper walked over and arched her back, rubbing against Kyle's leg. She circled him and wrapped her tail around his ankle. He knelt, offered his hand for her to sniff, and she gave him a solid headbutt on the hand. "Why thanks, Copper. I guess you're starting to like me," Kyle said. "Although, you are kind of disgusting right now and you've left something pretty nasty on my pant leg."

"What was that? What did he say?" asked Brock.

"I have no idea what he said, but that's how we cats tell

humans they're a member of our tribe. He may not know anything about the FLOCC, but I think he knows he's part of our team now."

Headbutts and Tail Rubs

Cats have scent glands located at different spots on their bodies, like the tops of their heads, their cheeks, and their tails. A cat's scent gland is an organ that releases a chemical called a pheromone. Humans can't see or smell those pheromones, but cats can easily detect their own scent as well as the scents of any other cats who have been around.

Our feline friends use their scent glands to leave their own personal smell on the humans, objects, and other cats that they encounter on a regular basis. Smell helps them to recognize familiar people and places, and it's one more way that cats communicate, along with their verbalizations and body language.

So, when a cat headbutts you, rubs its tail against you, or slides its cheek across the corner of your wall, it's saying it owns you and all your possessions. It's probably also telling you that it loves you because nothing says I love you like, "I just sprayed some invisible smelly stuff on you."

Learn more at distractfacts.com/headbutts.

As Kyle brushed the goo left by Copper off his pants, he heard a door slam across the parking lot. It was Julius Swine, heading out of his office after a very long evening on the night shift.

"Time to scatter! Unknown human on the way!" cried Big Strig.

"How am I going to get home?" asked Copper.

"Stick with the human," answered Riley. "He'll get you home one way or another."

Big Strig bounced toward Riley and grabbed the tree frog in his talons.

"But what do I do when I get home?" questioned Copper. "How will I know what to do next?"

"No need to worry! I'll be in touch!" Riley cried as he flew off in the clutches of the great horned owl.

Julius Swine gawked as a siege of black-crowned night herons ran into the bushes by the pond while crows and owls flew every which way. In the center of all the chaos, a grimy-looking cat meowed loudly at the feet of the young man who had been in his office earlier.

"Crazy night, huh, Mr. Swine?" asked Kyle with a broad, extra-toothy smile.

Swine offered no reply. He jumped into his car, locked the doors, and sped out of the parking lot as he swatted imaginary creatures off his shoulders.

"Well, that went smoothly," said Kyle. He opened the door to the tow truck and Copper bounded inside. "Sun's coming up, Copper. Let's get you home."

17

AN UNEXPECTED GUEST

Kyle climbed into the truck and wiped a speck of mud from the tag on Copper's collar. "It's a little early, but let's give your owners a call now in case they don't know you're gone yet. That'll save them from getting upset." After Kyle rolled up the windows, he dialed the number listed on her tag. "Hi, my name is Kyle Hammond, and I believe I've found your cat," Kyle explained as he glanced at Copper. She was sitting on the floorboard in ultimate cleaning mode once again.

"Yeah, I run Hammond's Auto Repair and Salvage and I found her in my junkyard last night. She seems just fine. I'd say she needs a bath but other than that, it doesn't look like she's hurt." Kyle cracked the truck windows and turned on the air vents; the cat reeked more than she had earlier, if that was even possible. "I'm already out on the road. I'll be glad to bring her to you if you'd like," he offered.

Kyle could not understand how on earth the cat could stand licking the nasty stuff that was covering her fur. As he took another peek at Copper, he felt a little nauseous. "Yep, I know where that is. Y'all aren't far from my shop. I should be there in about half an hour or so."

Kyle winced as Copper jumped on his seat to get some back support for her cleaning. He held the phone away from his face and whispered, "No-no! Get down!" The cat, for some reason, simply sped up her frenzied cleaning.

Turning his attention back to the phone, Kyle responded, "Oh—yes, you're welcome! Glad to help. See you soon. Bye." Kyle stifled a gag as he looked over at Copper again.

"Thanks to you, I'm going to have to leave the windows down in here for a week and get about six of those Christmas tree air fresheners," he said to Copper after ending the call. "I don't even know if a fire hose will get that funk off my seat."

"Can't talk. Cleaning," said Copper between licks.

Kyle wondered what the little chirrup sound meant; it was kind of like a half-meow. He knew it had to mean something. Those creatures who showed up in his junkyard had proven there was a meaning to the sights, sounds, and actions of all the living things around him. All he had to do was slow down to look and listen, and he could find amazing things he had never noticed before.

Dark sky faded to blue as the sun rose behind him. Lowering his window, Kyle inhaled the pungent, comforting smells of saltwater and marshy pluff mud as the truck crossed the rivers and creeks on the way to Copper's house. She stopped her cleaning more than once to get a whiff. Despite her best efforts, by the time they had reached her house, Copper had tongue-cleared only one little patch of fur on her belly. Kyle scrunched his nose and scooped her up like he was handling an armload of rotten fruit and carried her to the front door.

As if the doorbell was wired directly to a dog with a megaphone, an earsplitting bedlam of barking erupted inside the house when Kyle pressed the button. The noise was so irritating and shrieky, he considered setting Copper down and stuffing pine straw in his ears. He could not imagine why people would torture themselves by keeping an animal capable of such auditory abomination inside the confined space of a house. Even the cat looked like she was shaking her head in disgust.

The door was opened by a man who held the dog back with one leg, letting the bothersome barking blast down the street. Kyle half-expected car alarms to go off, flowers to wilt, and squirrels to dig up acorns to shove in their ears. "Hi, Mr. Catesby, I'm Kyle Hammond," he shouted as if he was standing next to the speakers at a Johnny Jones Johnson Junior concert. "I've brought your cat."

"Hi, Kyle, come on in," Mr. Catesby replied calmly. He had clearly built up some sort of tolerance to the dog's deafening yapping. "Don't mind Oscar. Once he gets a few sniffs of you, he'll calm down."

"If he gets a few sniffs of your cat, he might pass out," laughed Kyle.

Kyle set Copper down on the welcome mat, and the hoodie-wearing dog stopped barking while he sniffed and whined at her. Kneeling to greet Oscar, Kyle held out his hand so that the dog could get a whiff of his scent. As Oscar was calming down, two children came bounding down the stairs, followed by Mrs. Catesby, sending the dog into hiding under the coffee table.

"Copper's back!" the kids cheered and then both exclaimed, "Ewww! What happened to her?"

"She's obviously had herself an interesting time tonight," said Mrs. Catesby, examining Copper's appearance. "She's got mud everywhere, bits of fur missing from her tail and . . . are those bird feathers in her collar?"

"Mama, I want to be the one who gets to give her a bath."

"I don't see why not, Molly. It'll have to be a good one because she smells like a seafood market dumpster."

Sitting on the floor next to the filthy cat, Molly gently stroked Copper's chin. "What are those little brown flakes on her forehead?" asked Molly.

"They look like slivers of rusty metal," her father replied.

"Oh, that's probably from the tailpipe she had stuck on her face," said Kyle.

"Tailpipe?" the entire family exclaimed with head-tilts that would make Copper proud.

"Yeah, when I found her in my junkyard, she had a broken tailpipe stuck on her face and—" Kyle was trying to think of a way to explain finding her with all the other animals when he noticed the dog rolling something peculiar across the floor. "I think I might have something else that belongs to you," he said.

"Well, if it's a goat, it is definitely not ours," said Mr. Catesby.

Kyle did his own version of a Copper head-tilt. "Did you say goat?"

"Ha! It's a crazy story. You wouldn't believe me if I told you."

"I think I probably would. Be right back," said Kyle. He trotted out to his truck and returned with the plunger cup. "This was lying on the ground in my junkyard where I found your cat. I'm guessing it goes with that plunger stick your dog is rolling around."

"How in the world did it get to your junkyard?" asked Mr. Catesby.

Kyle remembered seeing the owl fly across the highway, carrying the cat with a plunger cup on its foot, and he tried to think of how to explain that. Luckily, the dog began to bark and whine again, saving him from having to explain that little scene.

"Mason, I think Oscar needs to go to the bathroom. Go ahead and turn his collar back on. I don't think the owls are coming back," said Mrs. Catesby.

Kyle chuckled as Mason switched on the collar. "Y'all saw the owls, too?"

Before anyone could answer, a sharp bark followed by a yelp at the doggy door made them all turn to look. Oscar had made it halfway out, but now he was coming back inside, retreating backwards through the doggy door. Surprisingly, a white calico cat with orange and black patches strutted into the house behind the dog.

"Oh no!" cried Copper. "It's Callie!"

Now safely back in the house, Oscar went into a frenzy of ear-piercing barking, jumping toward Callie and springing back again and again. Standing her ground, Callie hissed at the dog with such wildness it gave all the humans an instant outbreak of goose bumps. Then Oscar made the mistake of jumping a little too close, and Callie walloped him on the nose with a high-speed swat too fast to see even on a slow-motion replay.

Every creature in the room was shocked at Callie's grand entrance. The humans were shocked at the suddenness of the sweet, sweet quiet that fell on their ears with the abrupt stoppage of dog yapping. Copper was just shocked to see Callie suddenly standing in her living room. Oscar was shocked because it was his first introduction to Callie's Paw of Silence. It would not be his last. Oscar ran behind the couch to spend some time reconsidering his approach to greeting house guests.

"What does that dog have on it? What's it for?" Callie interrupted the silence with her usual croaky tone.

"It's a hoodie. It doesn't really have a—never mind," replied Copper, who then followed up with her own question. "What are you doing here?"

"Trust me, honey, this is the last place I want to be," said Callie. "There is so much cute in here it's making my stomach turn. Squeaky toys scattered everywhere, a plushy bed by the windowsill, and a play tower in the corner. This place would turn the strongest of cats into a sniveling weakling."

"Then why are you here? Did you know I'm part of the FLOCC now?"

"Yes, I heard, but I'm not here to deliver your first squad hug if that's what you think. I'm here on FLOCC business."

"What business is that?"

"A lot of what we do out in the field is dangerous," replied Callie. "The squeaky toys out there can bite you back. If you're going to join our missions, you need to toughen up. I'm here to give you some training."

"Look, Mama, they're meowing at each other," exclaimed Molly. "Maybe it's a friend Copper made while she was outside!"

"Stay back from her, kids. She seems like she might be rabid," warned Mr. Catesby.

"I don't think so," said Kyle. "I've seen this cat before. Just like Copper, I found it one day in my junkyard and the crows had me—I mean—I took it to the animal shelter. I don't think it could have rabies because they would have vaccinated it then. It's odd that it showed up here, though."

"It's been an odd kind of night around here," Mr. Catesby replied.

"Mama, if it's a stray, do you think we can keep it? Copper seems to like her," asked Mason.

"Yeah, wouldn't it be cool for Copper to have a friend to play with?" Molly agreed.

"I don't know about that kids," Mrs. Catesby replied as she watched the two cats. "Although, Copper does seem to be chatty with this cat, and it certainly isn't afraid of Oscar. We'll call the shelter when they open and find out what the story is with this kitty."

Both kids gave a celebratory fist pump.

"In the meantime," Mrs. Catesby continued, "take Copper upstairs and get her that bath."

Giving a huge yawn as he rolled his head from shoulder to shoulder, Kyle said, "It was very nice to meet you all. But it's been a long night and I think I'm going to go home and get some rest."

"Kyle, thank you so much for bringing Copper back to us," said Mr. Catesby. "Can we offer you anything for your trouble?"

"That won't be necessary. I'm happy I was able to help. Here's my business card if we need to get in touch again."

"Thank you, Kyle. You will definitely be our go-to guy for any car repairs or tow help we need."

Kyle shook hands with Mr. and Mrs. Catesby and headed out the door. Right before shutting it, he stuck his head back in. "Feel free to call me if you see that goat again. We might have some stories to share."

As the front door shut and Molly carried her up the stairs, Copper heard a sound that always made her cringe. Water was running into a tub, which meant a bath was coming. Normally, Copper would rather sit in a room with a hundred Yaps yapping than get a bath, but it was worth it this time. Looking down, over Molly's shoulder, she watched as Mason cautiously rubbed Callie on the head, both sitting at the base of the stairs. Yap crept out from behind the couch, with his tail wagging but his mouth shut. He started to growl a little; Callie lifted her paw ever so slightly.

The growling immediately stopped.

Copper didn't know what it would be like to have Callie living in the house or even how long Callie would stay, but she did know that it would be a lot quieter.

While Copper suffered through the indignity of being shampooed and rinsed in the bathtub, she replayed the night's events in her mind. She had always thought that it was simply adventure she craved, but now she realized that adventure was best when it had a purpose. She had learned her purpose was to help other creatures through her work with the FLOCC, and that her connection to humans would serve her well.

Although Riley had told her he'd be in touch, Copper was already anticipating what the next mission would be and when she would hear about it. No matter when or where the next adventure happened, it would probably start the way her first adventure had, with a green tree frog pressed against a pane of glass on her patio door.

The End . . .

THE TAXONOMY OF COPPER AND THE TREE FROG

NEVER CALL A GREAT HORNED OWL BIG BUBO

When Copper's adventures began at the Chucktown Cats & Hounds animal shelter, she didn't know her own name. Sarge explained to Copper that the humans who adopted her would also give her a name. Sarge knows that we humans love naming things. We even have a name for our science of naming living creatures, taxonomy, and we refer to the scientists who specialize in naming creatures as taxonomists.

You might be doing your own version of Copper's trademark head-tilt right now and asking the same question Copper might ask.

"Why are there scientists who specialize in naming things?"

Well, scientists need to ensure they're all referring to the same type of creature when they are doing their work.

The names most of us use for plants and animals are called common names. Domestic cat or American crow (or quite often just cat and crow) are examples of common names. Sometimes, common names can be confusing because people may use the same name for two different organisms. For example, if you told me you saw a daddy-long-legs, I would think you meant a spider-like arachnid that is also called a harvestman. (I learned about that one as a kid.) To other people, a daddy-long-legs is a different long-legged insect commonly known as a crane fly, and still others use that name to refer to a certain type of cellar spider. But if you said you saw a creature with the scientific name *Pholcus phalangioides*, then everyone would know you meant the cellar spider.

If Copper wasn't distracted by a field cricket with the scientific name *Gryllus rubens* right now, she'd probably want to know how the two words that make a creature's scientific name are picked. That's where the taxonomists come in. Scientific names are created by taxonomists, who use a two-word system called binomial nomenclature to give each kind of living organism a unique name. The two words used to make a scientific name are always Latin or Greek. Latin is useful because it's no longer spoken, so the meanings of Latin words can never change.

Taxonomists place organisms into categories based on traits the creatures have in common. The biggest category is called a domain, and all of the creatures Copper met in this adventure are part of a domain called Eukarya. Within a domain, there are categories called kingdoms. You probably already know at least two of those kingdoms, Animalia (animals) and Plantae (plants). Within a kingdom, scientists will then group an organism into a category called a phylum, then class, order, family, and genus. The rules taxonomists use for deciding which creatures go into each category can change as they learn more about the creatures and as new technology emerges.

All the creatures in a particular genus are very similar in some way. The field cricket that is currently distracting

Copper is part of a genus called *Gryllus,* which includes lots of similar looking crickets, but each is different somehow.

Now if Bart were here right now, he would have a very intense look on his face. Some things would probably be on his mind.

"What does *Gryllus* mean? Why is Copper's cricket called *Gryllus rubens?* And why do you keep writing the scientific name *like that?*"

As with everything in life, there is a rich story behind the answers to those questions. Gryllus is a Latin word that was used for crickets. The first word in a scientific name, also called the species name, is the creature's genus and it always starts with a capital letter, which is why Copper's cricket's name begins with *Gryllus.* The second word in a scientific name is called the specific epithet or specific name, and it is always written in lowercase letters. It's a word that distinguishes the creature from all the others in its genus. Copper's cricket is the type that tends to have reddish spots on its side and sometimes red-tinted legs. The Latin word rubens was used to describe something reddish in color, so the cricket with reddish-looking spots on its side that Copper is trying to catch was given the scientific name of *Gryllus rubens.* And the standard way to write scientific names is with *italics.* There is probably a story behind that standard, but there's no way we can keep Copper's attention long enough to dive into that.

Scientific names aren't always related to the way a creature looks, but there is a unique story behind every common name and every scientific name. Ravens like Linnaeus have the scientific name *Corvus corax,* a combination of the Latin word for raven (Corvus) and the Greek word for croaker (corax), the sound a raven makes. American crows like Brock and Harriet are called *Corvus brachyrhynchos* which combines the Latin word for raven with a Greek word for short-billed (brachyrhynchos). American crows have shorter bills than common ravens. Great horned owls like Big Strig have the scientific name of *Bubo virginianus.* Bubo is thought to be a Latin word for owl or horned owl, and virginianus means the person who named them first observed the owls in the state of Virginia.

Common names also have interesting origin stories. Crows probably get their name from the Old English word "crawe" which may have been an imitation of the sound of a crow's call. When Spanish explorers arrived in the New World, they encountered massive armored reptiles with thick, powerful tails and intimidating jaws packed with teeth. The explorers called these reptiles *el lagarto,* the lizard, but the English combined the two words and over time that led to the common name we use today for the alligator. Even your own name has a story behind it. It might be a family name that has been passed down to you, it might reflect a time of year or a place that was special to your parents, or maybe it is a name your parents read in a book and thought would be an awesome name for their child. No matter what, there's a great story behind your name.

So, just like you and all the living things in our world, I believe Copper and her friends deserve names that have special meanings and tell a story of their own. I thought you might be interested in those stories, so in this section I'm sharing the not-so-scientific meanings behind the names of Copper and her friends. I have also included their actual scientific names for you as well. I hope you enjoy the taxonomy of *Copper and the Tree Frog!* - Mike

COPPER (*FELIS CATUS*): Copper figured out the name that her humans gave her, but she still doesn't have any idea why they gave her that name. I tried to tell her the story, but she was too busy cleaning her shiny orange fur to listen. You can tell she spends a lot of time grooming because her fur gleams like a newly minted penny.

CALLIE (*FELIS CATUS*): Callie got her name because she's a Calico cat, but there was no way I was going to try telling that to Callie. I once made the mistake of commenting on that banana-shaped brown streak under her eye, and she introduced me to her Paw of Silence. If you want any more details about Callie's history, you'll have to hope Sarge lets the cat out of the bag on another of Copper's adventures.

SARGE (*FELIS CATUS*): Speaking of Sarge, he told Copper that his animal friends gave him his name years ago, but this isn't the first time I've heard of a cat named Sarge. One of Copper's humans, Mrs. Catesby, once said that the staff at the shelter where they adopted Copper had first given Copper the name Sarge. Of course, the Catesbys changed it once they adopted her, kind of like Sarge's human had given him a different name, as Callie mentioned. There's probably a story behind both of Sarge's names, but he doesn't really want to share those stories just yet.

THE CATESBY FAMILY, AKA COPPER'S HUMANS (*HOMO SAPIENS*): Copper's humans are the Catesby family, and I happen to have a few things in common with Mr. Catesby. He has two kids named Mason and Molly, which is an amazing coincidence because I also have two children named Mason and Molly. Mr. Catesby and I also share a love for nature. He's proud to be able to tell people how his family name, Catesby, is shared by Mark Catesby, a famous naturalist from England. Back in 1722, Mark Catesby arrived in Copper's hometown of Charleston, South Carolina to write a book which is considered the first illustrated publication describing the flora (plants) and fauna (animals) of North America. The book was titled *The Natural History of Carolina, Florida and the Bahama Islands*. Unlike Copper's Mr. Catesby, there are no records of Mark Catesby the English naturalist throwing plunger cups at great horned owls.

YAP AKA OSCAR (*CANIS LUPUS FAMILIARIS*): Even Yap's long scientific name involves more yapping than others, but like a lot of creatures, Yap has more than one common name or nickname. Copper gave Yap his nickname because of his vociferous yelping and yipping, and the Catesbys named him Oscar because one of the Catesby kids liked the name. I couldn't remember which kid picked the name, so I called Mr. Catesby. When he answered, the phone's ringing triggered the dog into a shockwave-inducing symphony of shrieking that shattered my cellphone screen. I'll try again after I get my phone repaired . . . perhaps when I know Callie is nearby.

RILEY (*HYLA CINEREA*): You might be surprised to find out that even though it seems like every creature in the Charleston area knows Riley, none of them has a clue as to how the most popular green tree frog in town got his name. One person I haven't asked yet is Joe Riley. He was the mayor of Charleston for about forty years, so I'm sure he and Riley the tree frog had to have met at some point.

BART (*STRIX VARIA*): I once read that the man who wrote the Declaration of Independence, Thomas Jefferson, was friends with a naturalist named Benjamin Smith Barton, the man who first published a description of the barred owl. I thought this was an interesting fact to share with Bart since he's a barred owl. I joked about how Bart and Barton sounded similar, so maybe he was named after the person who had already given him a name. Bart hasn't responded yet, but he's got an intense look on his face that makes me believe he's thinking about it.

BIG STRIG (*BUBO VIRGINIANUS*): Big Strig isn't an owl of many words, so he's not likely to tell you much of a story if you ask him about the meaning behind his name. The "Big" part is obvious. Great horned owls are large owls, and Big Strig is huge even for a great horned owl. But what about that Strig part? It reminds me of *Strigidae*, the family name for owls like Big Strig and Bart. A family name is one of those taxonomy categories that scientists use to group similar creatures. Even though Big Strig and Bart are different enough to have separate genus categories, *Strix* for Bart and *Bubo* for Big Strig, all *Strix* and *Bubo* owls are considered part of the true owl family named *Strigidae*. I can see why Big Strig went with his family name instead of his genus. Big Bubo doesn't sound nearly as tough, but it does sound like something Bart would call him. From a distance.

RAM (*CAPRA HIRCUS*): As Riley very clearly explained, Ram is called Ram because he likes to ram stuff. A ram is the name for a male sheep, but Ram is a goat, not a sheep. Lucky for y'all, that's not confusing at all.

BROCK (*CORVUS BRACHYRHYNCHOS*): I figured if any of Copper's friends already knew the story behind their own name, it would be an intelligent crow like Brock. When I asked him, he confirmed that he knew the story, but he wouldn't tell it to me. He said he had his doubts about why I was asking. I guess he needs more time to get to know me. During our conversation, Harriet was by his side as always, and she correctly explained that Brock was short for the second part of his scientific name, the specific epithet *brachyrhynchos*. Yes, I know Brock is spelled differently. If that is the kind of thing that bothers you, you just might be a future taxonomist!

HARRIET (*CORVUS BRACHYRHYNCHOS*): After I thanked Harriet for rescuing me from my awkward conversation with Brock, I told her the name Harriet always made me think of Harriet Lawrence Hemenway. Back in the late 1800s, many women enjoyed wearing fancy hats decorated with feathers from birds. The hat companies often obtained the feathers from people who had killed thousands of birds, like the snowy egret, to get the feathers. Harriet Hemenway and her cousin, Minna Hall, wanted to do something to stop the killing of birds for fashion. They started a group encouraging women to stop buying hats decorated with feathers, and about 900 women joined the team. Eventually, laws were passed to prevent the killing of so many birds for fashion. Harriet's organization grew into the National Audubon Society which protects birds all over the country. I got so caught up in telling Harriet the crow about Harriet Hemenway, I forgot to ask her if she knew the story behind her own name.

JOHNNY JONES JOHNSON JUNIOR (*HOMO SAPIENS*): Johnny Jones Johnson Junior is an international country music superstar, so he's not the type of person you can just call to have a discussion about the meaning of his name. Fortunately, everyone already knows the story behind his name. Johnny Jones Johnson Junior was named after his father, Johnny Jones Johnson Senior.

LINNAEUS (*CORVUS CORAX*): While just about everyone recognizes a famous name like Johnny Jones Johnson Junior, not as many people have heard of a Swedish scientist named Carl Linnaeus who lived in the 1700s. He was the founder of the current binomial (two-name) naming system used for giving organisms their scientific names and is often referred to as the Father of Taxonomy. Linnaeus gave scientific names, which are still in use today, for thousands of species, including common ravens. Perhaps Linnaeus the raven got his name from Linnaeus the taxonomist. If we ever get to meet Linnaeus, maybe he'll tell us.

BENNY (*NYCTICORAX NYCTICORAX*): The first time I ever saw a black-crowned night heron was on one of my lunchtime walks. I was leaning against a wooden railing by a lagoon at a local resort and watching a snowy egret as it waded in the water. Suddenly, I realized there was a bird perched as still as a statue in the bushes right in front of me. It looked like a small heron with brown wings and white speckles all over it. I took a picture of course, and after checking my field guide later, I discovered it was a juvenile black-crowned night heron. Each day I walked by, it seemed like that same bird was standing there in the same spot. My kids started calling him Benny. What a coincidence that Copper's new black-crowned night heron friend is also named Benny! But after Benny explained how often he has named one of his chicks Benny Jr., I realized this coincidence wasn't as remarkable as I'd originally thought. It seems to be a popular name amongst black-crowned night herons.

JULIUS SWINE (*HOMO SAPIENS*): After a stop for a pulled pork sandwich at one of my favorite local barbeque restaurants, I visited the owner of the Hog Island Resort, Julius Swine. I asked him if he could slice off a strip of time to talk about the sizzling story behind the meaning of his name. I don't know if I just caught him at a bad time, or if he thought I was a bit of a boar for asking, but he wouldn't answer me. He kept swatting at his back like there was an invisible tree frog on it. He was at work, so I suspect he was preoccupied with getting his job done and bringing home the bacon. I'm sure I'll see him again, so I'll try to get him to squeal some details when his focus is a little crisper.

ELLIOTT (*STRIX VARIA*): I haven't talked to Bart's dad, Elliott, since he went back to his forest, but for some reason I was thinking of him recently when I drove past one of my favorite places to visit around Charleston. It's called The Center for Birds of Prey and it was founded by a man named James Elliott. The Center provides medical care for injured birds of prey, conducts educational programs about the birds, and even does flight demonstrations with eagles, owls, falcons, and more. The Center for Birds of Prey is an amazing place for humans and birds alike. I have a feeling Bart's dad would really like it.

BELLE (*STRIX VARIA*): The same day I drove north along the coast and saw The Center for Birds of Prey, I also passed by another marvelous place called Hobcaw Barony. It's a vast nature preserve and research center that was owned by a woman named Belle Baruch. Miss Baruch wanted to ensure her property stayed undisturbed for the many plants and animals in the forests and wetlands there, so she set up a foundation to protect it. Much like Bart's mama, Belle, I think Belle Baruch would have been a good candidate for the FLOCC.

BILL FOWLER (*HOMO SAPIENS*): Meteorologists do valuable work, and Charleston's annual hurricane season is always a reminder of how important their weather forecasts are to everyone. Two of the great long-time meteorologists in Charleston are Rob Fowler and Bill Walsh. I don't know if they've met the new guy, Bill Fowler, but I don't think I can trust the Wizard of Weather's coin flip when I need to know if the next hurricane is going to hit us.

KYLE HAMMOND (*HOMO SAPIENS*): Nobody in the FLOCC has known Kyle longer than Ram, so I thought he would want to share the story behind Kyle's name. Ram answered in his usual manner:

> We knew a boy so dreadful sick;
> It seemed like such an awful trick.
> His family ached to hold him longer,
> But Heaven's call was even stronger.
> And then another boy fell ill,
> The kind for which there is no pill.
> His family fought to get him well,
> But he, too, with the angels dwells.

Two families we consider friends,
Whose sorrow seems to know no end.
We hope these words will help them smile,
To know one was Hammond, the other
   Kyle.

ACKNOWLEDGMENTS

The story of the journey to get this book into your hands could perhaps fill a book on its own although I doubt it would be as exciting as getting a ride from a great horned owl with a plunger cup stuck on your foot.

Like Copper, I had help from a few friends on my adventure. I am grateful to my editor, Dr. Laura Rotta, for her valiant efforts to clean up the mess left behind in the wake of my crimes against the English language. She fought the good fight, and any issues that remain were a result of changes I made while she had her back turned. Leysan Sovetnikova's beautiful illustrations help to bring Copper and her friends to life and spare you the horror of having to look at my stick figure art. My beta readers, the Jordan family and the Krabbenhoft family, helped to keep me on track toward the goal of writing a book that kids and their grown-ups would enjoy. I am most grateful for my family, Monica, Mason, and Molly, who listened to fresh chapters at the dinner table, laughed at all the right times, supported me and encouraged me throughout the journey, and taped motivational cat posters on the wall in my office. You gave me the inspiration to write the story, and you gave me the strength to finish it.

Finally, I'm grateful to each reader, for taking your time to dive into the world of *Copper and the Tree Frog* with me. I hope that it has inspired you to get outside to experience what the natural world has to offer. There are real-life magical creatures right outside all our doors. And whether it is now or in the years to come, if you have a story you'd like to tell, then I encourage you with all my heart to press on and get that story out into the world. There will be mountains to climb and bogs to slog, but be strong and courageous, for you are never alone. There is always at least one caring creature somewhere nearby, willing to help and rooting for you. When you look, you see.

ABOUT THE AUTHOR

As a highly-decorated, frequently-disciplined former class clown, Mike Jones has always thought we can laugh and learn at the same time. He is a member of the Children & Nature Network and a Coastal Master Naturalist living in Charleston, South Carolina with his wife, two kids, an orange tabby cat named Copper, and enough tree frogs to qualify as a biblical plague. Mike believes that we can tell stories that are funny, educational, exciting, and meaningful, all in one package. You can find him online at mikejoneswrites.com.

facebook.com/mikejoneswrites
twitter.com/mikejoneswrites
instagram.com/mikejoneswrites

COMING FALL 2020!

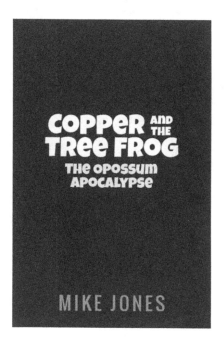

What dangers will Copper face on her next mission? And how disgusting will her fur get along the way? You can ask your grown-ups to sign up at copperandthetreefrog.com to get notified of the official release date for Copper's next adventure, *Copper and the Tree Frog: The Opossum Apocalypse*!

And if your grown-ups have time, let Mike know what you thought about *Copper and the Tree Frog: The Night Heron Nabbing* by leaving a short review on Amazon or your other preferred store. It helps other parents and children find the story. Thank you!

CPSIA information can be obtained
at www.ICGtesting.com
Printed in the USA
LVHW111449220721
693423LV00009B/460/J

9 780989 004640